D1141073

The British Cookbook

The British Cookbook

THE BEST OF BRITISH FOOD

This edition published in 2010
LOVE FOOD is an imprint of Parragon Books Ltd

Parragon
Queen Street House
4 Queen Street
Bath BA1 1HE, UK

Copyright © Parragon Books Ltd 2007

LOVE FOOD and the accompanying heart device is a registered trade mark of Parragon Books Ltd in Australia, the UK, US and the EU.

All rights reserved. No part of this publication may be reproduced, stored in a retrieval system, or transmitted, in any form or by any means, electronic, mechanical, photocopying, recording, or otherwise, without the prior permission of the copyright holder.

ISBN: 978-1-4454-0360-1

Printed in China

Internal design by Talking Design
Photography by Mike Cooper
Home economy by Lincoln Jefferson
Recipes by Pamela Gwyther
Introduction by Beverly Le Blanc

Notes for the Reader

This book uses metric and imperial measurements. Follow the same units of measurement throughout; do not mix metric and imperial. All spoon measurements are level: teaspoons are assumed to be 5 ml, and tablespoons are assumed to be 15 ml. Unless otherwise stated, milk is assumed to be full fat, eggs and individual vegetables are medium, and pepper is freshly ground black pepper.

The times given are an approximate guide only. Preparation times differ according to the techniques used by different people and the cooking times may also vary from those given. Optional ingredients, variations, or serving suggestions have not been included in the calculations.

Recipes using raw or very lightly cooked eggs should be avoided by infants, the elderly, pregnant women, convalescents and anyone suffering from an illness. Pregnant and breastfeeding women are advised to avoid eating peanuts and peanut products. Sufferers from nut allergies should be aware that some of the ready-made ingredients used in the recipes in this book may contain nuts. Always check the packaging before use.

Picture Acknowledgements

The publisher would like to thank the following for permission to reproduce copyright material: Cover: British flag © Garry Gay/Getty Images; Knife, Fork and plate © Geir Pettersen/Getty Images. Internals: Simon Wilkinson/Iconica/Getty Images (page 8); Peter Adams/Taxi/Getty Images (page 11); Neil Beer/Photodisc/Getty Images (page 12); Anthony-Masterson/The Image Bank/Getty Images (page 13); Jeremy Walker/The Image Bank/Getty Images (page 14); Anthony-Masterson/The Image Bank/Getty Images (page 15); Simon Wilkinson/Iconica/Getty Images (page 16); Amy Neunsinger/The Image Bank/ Getty Images (page 18).

CONTENTS

INTRODUCTION

Traditional home cooking from England, Wales, Scotland and Northern Ireland has never been totally forgotten, although it has often had to play second fiddle to many food fads over the years. Fortunately, it is now enjoying a revival and cooks everywhere are remembering the joys of eating British food. It is hearty, often filling and, most important of all, flavoursome. This is why many of the recipes in this collection have been passed down through the generations. Quality, fresh ingredients are the backbone of British cooking. British cooks have almost always been blessed with great variety and choice and the recipes in this collection reflect this abundance. Enjoy savouring the flavours of Britain.

'MANY FAVOURITE DISHES TODAY HAVE THEIR ORIGINS IN SIMPLE AGRICULTURAL AND COOKING PRACTICES OF PAST GENERATIONS'

This recipe collection is a celebration of traditional British food and cooking, and you'll find our food heritage is as diverse and interesting as Britons themselves. Many favourite dishes today have their origins in simple agricultural and cooking practices of past generations and are influenced by the flavourings and ingredients that have been absorbed and adopted from foreign countries. The ability of British chefs to constantly evolve has given us a culinary repertoire in which spiced dishes, such as Kedgeree and Mulligatawny Soup, sit happily alongside Roast Beef and Yorkshire Pudding. These are all part of the exciting, flavoursome mix that is British food.

What is British Food?

British food is both simple and sophisticated, but many traditional favourites recall harsher times. Lancashire hotpot, Irish stew and shepherd's pie, for example, are inexpensive dishes intended to fill up farm or factory workers, while leaving the cook free to get on with other chores. Yet, at the other end of the social scale, rich, indulgent dishes such as omelette Arnold Bennett began life in the kitchens of London's luxurious Savoy Hotel. British food has always had something to satisfy everyone and food fashions have never stood still, many coming full circle today. In the nineteenth century, for example, Scottish servants protested against being fed oysters every evening, as the molluscs were one of the cheapest ingredients available. Until recently, they still commanded premium prices because of their scarcity, but nowadays oyster farming makes them an affordable ingredient.

After foreign travel was embraced in the Sixties it became faddish to favour one foreign cuisine after another, often leaving traditional British food off menus. At last,

however, British food is enjoying a revival with many cooks returning to their culinary roots. Celebrity chefs have rekindled interest in preparing delicious home-cooked meals, and we are discovering the joys of cooking using seasonal, local ingredients. New cooks are also learning a basic lesson their great-grandparents considered second nature – seasonal ingredients are best and cheapest. For example, Brussels sprouts reach their flavour peak in the winter months and strawberries are at their most luscious and plentiful in the summer. Eating in tune with the seasons goes hand in hand with traditional British cooking – winter root vegetables are the staple of warming stews and casseroles while summer meals tend to be lighter, with greater emphasis on fresh salad items and fruits.

The great British food revival is also being promoted by a new generation of professional chefs. These enthusiastic cooks are breathing fresh life into humdrum and mediocre pub kitchens. Gastropubs rival traditional restaurants as the places to go for good, but relaxed, dining. Traditional pub favourites – chicken liver pâté, steak and kidney pie, beef stew with dumplings, and sausages and mash, to name a few – are back on the menu, sitting comfortably alongside the more exotic stir-fries and curries.

Consumers are also playing their part in the exciting food revival. Increased concern over the environmental costs of producing and transporting fresh produce means that customers want to know where their food comes from and how it has been produced. There is also a widening appreciation of organically produced food, boosting farmers' markets, delicatessens and specialist food shops.

Celebrating with British Food

Just as eating seasonally gives a sense of the passage of time, many British dishes are closely linked with secular and religious celebrations throughout the year. In Scotland, for example, where the new year is ushered in with Hogmanay, the first-footer arrives with a piece of coal, bread and whisky, representing mankind's need for warmth, food and comfort. On 25 January, no Burns Night dinner, to honour the Scottish poet, is complete without haggis, neeps and tatties.

Since medieval times, when cream, eggs and milk were forbidden during Lent, pancakes are served on Shrove Tuesday to use up supplies in the larder before fasting begins the next morning, on Ash Wednesday. Pancake-tossing races are still enjoyed in many communities.

Mothering Sunday also has it origins in medieval times, not as a celebration of motherhood, but rather as a mid-Lent break, when church rules required priests and lay people to return to their mother church for worship. As this eventually evolved into a day of feasting, Simnel cake became part of the celebrations. The dense fruitcake, as baked today, contains a layer of rich marzipan through the centre and another layer on the top, with eleven marzipan balls representing Jesus' disciples, minus Judas.

Many foods are associated with Easter celebrations. Hot cross buns, lightly spiced and topped with dough crosses, are a Good Friday tradition. Since ancient times, eggs have been a symbol of continuing life, and brightly dyed and decorated hard-boiled Easter eggs have evolved out of that belief, with egg-rolling races symbolizing celebration of the returning sun and spring. (It was said the first boy and girl to get their eggs to the bottom of a hill would marry.) For the actual Easter day meal, spring food takes pride of place, and roast lamb with seasonal herbs, such as mint and parsley, is a popular choice. Baked custards were once a regular part of the Easter feast, celebrating the end of the prohibition on eggs and cream.

'WIMBLEDON JUST WOULDN'T SEEM COMPLETE WITHOUT BOWLS OF JUICY STRAWBERRIES'

As spring gives way to summer, tennis at the All-England Lawn Tennis and Croquet Club, in Wimbledon, just wouldn't seem complete without bowls of juicy strawberries and cream. Summer pudding, with its bread casing, isn't part of specific holiday observances, but rather a celebration of the season's glorious soft fruit.

When the weather cools and it's time to remember Guy Fawkes on the fifth of November, Bonfire Night parties demand warming food – hot, spiced cider, jacket potatoes and parkin, a sticky ginger cake from northern England, for example. Halloween, from the religious observance of All Hallows' Eve, or All Saints' Day, is now frequently combined with Bonfire Night celebrations, adding toffee apples to the menu.

As British cooks' attentions turn towards Christmas, Stir-up Sunday, the second Sunday in Advent, is the traditional time to make the Christmas pudding, with each family member giving the thick batter a stir. In the West Country and throughout the south-east, with the many apple orchards, wassailing is a long-established tradition on Christmas Eve, or St Stephen's feast day. Throughout British history, the Christmas Day feast is the peak of the culinary year. Turkey or goose might provide the main course for many families today, but over the centuries boars' heads, venison, peacocks and roast beef have all been favoured. Mince pies have been part of the festivities since Elizabethan times.

The Best of British

Regional specialities, reflecting local geography and socio-economic history, provide the joy of British culinary traditions. Wherever you travel, you will find local specialities.

East Anglia

The gentle, undulating farmlands of East Anglia that stretch as far as the eye can see across low-lying, distant horizons, combined with a relatively dry climate, give the nation much of its soft fruit, wheat, barley, golden rape and sugar beet, as well as salad greens and apples.

This is also where much of the nation's poultry is raised, including the tender Norfolk Bronze turkey that graces many Christmas tables.

Some of the finest shellfish, including cockles, crabs, mussels, oysters, prawns, shrimp and whelks, come from here, along with cod, haddock, plaice, sole and turbot. Cromer crabs, from Norfolk, are heavy for their small size, which instantly lets you know they are packed with succulent meat. Herring have always been landed here, and small smokers produce kippers and bloaters to keep an ancient tradition alive.

The Midlands

Once Britain's industrial powerhouse, today the Midlands is a centre of agricultural activity. Hereford beef is enjoyed all over the country, and the red soil in parts of the region is ideal for apple and pear orchards and soft fruit, stone fruit and vegetables in abundance. One great seasonal treat is when the Vale of Evesham's asparagus appears in markets. Try asparagus with melted butter to appreciate the fine flavour.

Blue Stilton, labelled 'the king of British

'STILTON, LABELLED "THE KING OF CHEESES", MUST BE PRODUCED WITHIN THE BOUNDARIES OF DERBYSHIRE, LEICESTERSHIRE AND NOTTINGHAMSHIRE'

cheeses', must be produced within the boundaries of Derbyshire, Leicestershire and Nottinghamshire. Its international reputation, however, often overshadows the region's other noteworthy cheeses, such as Cheshire, Sage Derby, Red Leicester and Shropshire Blue.

The picturesque market town of Melton Mowbray is home to the uniquely British, eponymous pork pie, with its crisp hot-water crust and spiced filling.

Worcestershire sauce, one of the world's favourite savoury flavourings, began life in the 1830s as a mistake by chemists Mr Lea and Mr Perrins.

There have always been fine bakers in the Midlands, and Bakewell tart, with its creamy almond-flavoured filling, is a great regional teatime treat.

The North

Food from this vast region, stretching from the Midlands north to the Scottish Borders, is traditionally hearty and filling.

Lancashire hotpot, a one-pot dish of lamb chops and root vegetables, was once only considered suitable for family meals, but now appears on restaurant menus. For another taste of no-frills northern cooking, try toad in the hole. And, of course, there is its cousin, Yorkshire pudding, the light, fluffy baked batter dish served alongside roast beef that was once a first course intended to fill up diners so less meat was required. The northern cook's reputation for frugality can still be glimpsed today when tripe and onions are served.

Vast grasslands, much on rugged terrain, support cattle and sheep, providing meat as well as excellent dairy products. Northern butchers pride themselves on their black puddings, as well as other offal preparations, and meat pies sold hot for eating on the spot or taking away. Dry-cured York ham, with its distinctive golden crumb coating, must be smoked over oak within 2 miles of York to be considered authentic. On the other side of the Pennines, mounded coils of Cumberland sausages are recognizable in butcher's-shop windows.

The long tradition of fishing along both coasts today faces shrinking stocks and economic pressure, but it still provides herring, whitefish and shellfish. The tiny brown shrimp and cockles from Morecambe Bay are considered a delicacy. Freshwater char, similar to salmon, is a spring favourite around Lake Windermere, in the Lake District.

Crumbly, white Lancashire cheese, with its salty flavour, is a regional favourite. Try a slice of unpasteurized Lancashire with an Eccles cake (spiced currants encased in puff pastry) for an intriguing and delicious end to a meal. Other regional cheeses worth looking for include Cotherstone and Wensleydale.

'MANY FISH ARE CAUGHT IN SCOTLAND'S LOCHS, RIVERS AND SURROUNDING WATERS, BUT SALMON AND HERRING ARE THE BEST KNOWN'

Northern Ireland

There is more to the Northern Irish diet than just potatoes, although it's rare to eat a meal here without them. Cultivated since the 1600s, potatoes were a subsistence crop in hard times, but today they take their place alongside simple but delicious lamb, pork, beef and plenty of seafood dishes.

Boom times in Belfast have kindled a renewed interest in traditional food and cooking, with artisan producers and cooks striving to put the region on Britain's culinary map. Yet, traditional favourites, such as Irish stew, are not forgotten. This one-pot meal typifies the region's cooking at its best. Colcannon – mashed potatoes with cabbage or kale, flavoured with creamy butter – is another example of simple everyday fare.

Pig farmers provide all of Britain with bacon, smoked and green, as well as flavoured with various cures.

River fishing is a popular sport, and cooks benefit from it with a good supply of trout, salmon, perch and pike. Fishing off the coast also provides cod, plaice and skate, as well as fresh prawns and oysters.

Northern Ireland has a tradition of home baking, and Irish soda bread has always been the cook's favourite because it is so quick to mix and bake.

Scotland

From the gentle, rolling Borders to the soaring Highlands and the Islands, Scotland yields a bountiful selection of ingredients that are any cook's delights. Scottish smoked salmon, Highland cattle, game and luscious ruby raspberries are valued by cooks throughout Britain. Yet, perhaps the country's best-known 'ingredients' are the numerous Scotch whiskies, sipped and savoured around the world.

Many fish are caught in Scotland's lochs, rivers and surrounding waters, but salmon and herring are the best known. Both have an oily flesh that lends itself to hot and cold smoking – Arbroath smokies, Finnan haddock and kippers are examples of Scottish smoked herring. Smoked haddock, another Scottish favourite, is the essential ingredient for omelette Arnold Bennett.

Aberdeen Angus, a popular breed of cattle that endures the harsh grazing conditions of northern Scotland, is highly valued in top kitchens everywhere. Deer are also adept at surviving in the Highlands, and the lean meat is ideal for venison casserole. Feathered game and wild hare are also popular, and game pie is a regular feature on menus during the season, beginning on the 'Glorious Twelfth' of August when grouse season opens. Haggis is a uniquely Scottish favourite, served with neeps and tatties.

Scotland also has a long tradition of cheese-making. Lanark Blue, made from sheep's milk, has a tangy flavour. Dunlop is the Scottish version of Cheddar, and Caboc is a very rich, soft cheese rolled in oatmeal.

London and the South

Despite the domination of bustling London and densely populated commuter towns, the Home Counties and the south-east contain a great deal of agricultural land, supplying the capital and the rest of the country with orchard fruit, soft fruit, vegetables, meat and dairy products. Wine and beer producers are also established in the region.

Many of Britain's favourite eponymous ingredients, products and dishes come from this region – Aylesbury ducks, Chelsea buns, Eton mess, Oxford marmalade, Sussex pond pudding and Whitstable oysters.

Kent, with its moist climate and rich soil, is known as the 'garden of England' and numerous varieties of apples and pears, hops and cob nuts grow here. Wild mushrooms from the New Forest are a seasonal delicacy.

Fishmongers here have plenty to offer from the Channel that winds southward from the Thames Estuary. Capture the flavour of a seaside holiday with fish and chips, which followed cockneys out of London.

London's contributions to Britain's culinary history are unmistakable. Since medieval times, chefs in the capital's public eating houses (publica coquina) have been setting the standards that eventually are adopted throughout the country. London's docks are also where many culinary treasures of the world entered Britain, adding extra flavour to home-grown produce.

Wales

When you think of Wales it is impossible not to think of the flocks of lamb in the harsh, mountainous landscape dotted with hill farms in the north.

Welsh food is traditionally simple, with plenty of richness added by butter, cheese and cream. For a taste of Wales, start with leek and potato soup, showcasing the iconic vegetable symbol of Wales, followed by roast leg of lamb with roast potatoes.

Seaweed is a regional delicacy from around the Gower Peninsula. Laverbread – purple laver seaweed picked from the rocks and cooked until it becomes a dark green, spinach-like mass, then rolled in oatmeal and fried – has never fallen out of favour. It can be an acquired taste, but complements sizzling bacon for a traditional breakfast.

Welsh bara brith, literally 'speckled bread', is a fruitcake laced with spices and studded with currants and raisins. It is delicious spread with creamy, salty butter at teatime.

'ABUNDANT ORCHARDS PROVIDE APPLES NOT ONLY FOR EATING AND BAKING, BUT ALSO FOR MAKING CIDER, THE REGION'S SIGNATURE DRINK'

The West Country

For many cooks, the West Country offers the best of land and sea. Cooks are literally spoilt for choice here.

Abundant orchards provide apples not only for eating and baking, but also for making cider, the region's signature drink.

Somerset is home to Cheddar, the world's favourite cheese, which has been made since the twelfth century. Other notable West Country cheeses include Double and Single Gloucester, Devon Garland and Cornish Yarg. This is also the only part of Britain where the dairy industry produces the ultra-indulgent clotted cream.

Wiltshire has a long tradition of pig farming, and 'Wiltshire cure' is a mild flavouring for bacon. The good news for carnivores is that the once almost-extinct Gloucester Old Spot pigs, with tender, succulent meat, are raised here.

Cornish pasties, originally baked as a portable, edible lunchbox for tin miners, remain a popular lunch or snack with holidaymakers and locals alike.

The picturesque coastline has long been popular with sailors (and smugglers!), surfers and walkers, and it yields excellent seafood. Daily catches include mackerel, monkfish, John Dory, sea bass and fine flatfish, along with crabs, lobsters and scallops. Freshwater fish, such as salmon, are also popular. Potted crab is a regular feature on the menus in the numerous habour-side restaurants along the coast.

The region's seafaring history made it a gateway for exotic spices, so it's not unusual to find ginger and saffron flavouring baked goods today, such as saffron cakes.

BRITISH SEASONAL FOOD
Use this handy guide to savour the best of the seasons with British ingredients. Here's what to look for each month:

JANUARY	Jerusalem artichokes, beetroot, Brussels sprouts, partridges, pheasants, wild duck, scallops
FEBRUARY	Carrots, cauliflower, celeriac, pork, veal, halibut, mussels, oysters, scallops
MARCH	Broccoli, cucumbers, kale, watercress, cooking and dessert apples, pears, salmon, salmon trout, skate
APRIL	Chinese leaves, cucumbers, lettuce, mint, parsley, radishes, spring onions, tomatoes, brill, mackerel, oysters, pork
MAY	Asparagus, endive, peppers, peas, spring onions, apricots, gooseberries, strawberries, crab, lobster, turbot, spring lamb
JUNE	Globe artichokes, asparagus, broad and kidney beans, marrows, new potatoes, black-/redcurrants, cherries, loganberries, plums, raspberries, strawberries, mullet, plaice, spring lamb, pork
JULY	Celery, courgettes, endive, greengages, mulberries, peaches, strawberries, brill, halibut, lobster, mullet, whitebait, venison
AUGUST	Calabrese broccoli, pumpkin, radishes, sweetcorn, tomatoes, turnips, damsons, gooseberries, greengages, plums, raspberries, rhubarb, strawberries, haddock, hake, trout, turbot, grouse, venison
SEPTEMBER	Beetroots, parsnips, maincrop potatoes, swedes, sweetcorn, tomatoes, elderberries, lobster, pike, hare, partridge, wild duck
OCTOBER	Celeriac, turnips, cooking and dessert apples, blackberries, black-/redcurrants, crab apples, chestnuts, medlars, quinces, strawberries, dab, mussels, oysters, beef, pheasant, wild duck
NOVEMBER	Jerusalem artichokes, carrots, kale, leeks, quinces, scallops, rabbit, turkey
DECEMBER	Brussels sprouts, cauliflower, swedes, watercress, cooking and dessert apples, chestnuts, halibut, herring, pike, skate, turkey, venison

1 BRITISH BREAKFASTS

Long, leisurely breakfasts might be a custom of the past, as everyone rushes to get out of the house in the morning, but eating breakfast every day is one of the most important steps to a healthy diet. There are plenty of British favourites that set you up for the day and don't take long to prepare. Porridge keeps you fuelled all morning and gives you a healthy start to the day. Classic Orange Marmalade & Toast is a zesty way to begin the day and eggs – cooked any way you like – are the original fast food. On weekends, try lightly curried Kedgeree, Welsh Rarebit or Potato Cakes for a lazy brunch.

CLASSIC ORANGE MARMALADE & TOAST

The British breakfast table doesn't seem complete without a jar of glistening orange marmalade. Once a luxury, because oranges were an expensive imported ingredient, marmalade has been a British favourite for several centuries. This traditional recipe, with thin strips of blanched orange peel, is made with Seville oranges. These oranges, in season in January and February, are too bitter for eating, but make wonderful marmalade. Buy lots when you see them so you can enjoy home-made marmalade throughout the year.

MAKES ABOUT 4.5 KG/10 LB

INGREDIENTS

1.5 kg/3 lb 5 oz Seville oranges, scrubbed
juice from 2 large lemons
3.4 litres/6 pints water
2.7 kg/6 lb preserving sugar
slices of thick white or brown bread, to serve

1 Cut the oranges in half and squeeze out all the juice. Scoop out all the pips from the orange shells and tie them up in a small piece of muslin. Slice the peel into small chunks or strips and place in a preserving pan together with the orange and lemon juice and water. Add the bag of pips.

2 Simmer gently for 1½ hours, or until the peel is very soft and the liquid has reduced by half. Remove the bag of pips, carefully squeezing to remove any juice. Add the sugar and heat, stirring, until the sugar has completely dissolved.

3 Bring to the boil and boil rapidly for about 15 minutes, or until the setting point is reached. Test if it is set by using a sugar thermometer. When it reads 105°C/221°F it is at a good setting point. Alternatively, test by dropping a small spoonful of marmalade onto a cold saucer, refrigerate to cool, then push it with a clean finger. If it forms a wrinkled skin it is ready. If not, boil the marmalade for a further minute and repeat.

4 Leave to cool slightly, then pot into warmed sterilized jars and cover the tops with waxed discs. When completely cold, cover with cellophane or lids, label and store in a cool place.

5 To serve, toast the bread on both sides under a medium grill or in a toaster. Spread thickly with the marmalade.

COOK'S TIP
Seville oranges freeze well, so if you don't have time to make a year's supply of marmalade, buy the oranges when they are in season and freeze for use later in the year.

FULL ENGLISH BREAKFAST

This is surely the best-known British dish of all! If we are to 'eat breakfast like a king, lunch like a gentleman and supper like a pauper', then this is the meal to kick-start the day. For most people, however, a 'full English' every day is too much, so this is a dish best prepared at the weekend after a night out and with plenty of time to cook and enjoy it. Personally, I prefer my English breakfast as brunch, with all morning – and all afternoon if I want – to eat and to read the papers.

SERVES 1

INGREDIENTS
2 good-quality pork sausages
2–3 smoked back bacon rashers
1 egg
1 slice 2-day-old wholemeal
   bread (optional)
1 large tomato, halved
vegetable oil, to drizzle
2–3 mushrooms
salt and pepper

1 Place the sausages under a hot grill and grill for about 15–20 minutes, turning frequently, until they are well browned.

2 Meanwhile, place the bacon rashers in a dry frying pan and fry for 2–4 minutes on each side, depending on how crisp you like your bacon. Remove from the frying pan, leaving all the excess bacon fat, and keep the bacon warm. The frying pan can then be used to fry the egg if you choose
to have it fried. (See page 32: Ways with Eggs.)

3 Alternatively, use the delicious bacon fat to make fried bread. Heat the frying pan and place the bread in the fat. Cook for 1–2 minutes on one side, then turn over and repeat. Do not cook too quickly or the bread will burn.

4 The tomato halves can be placed under the hot grill with the sausages. Drizzle with a little oil and season to taste with salt and pepper before grilling for 3–4 minutes.

5 The mushrooms can be grilled with the tomatoes or quickly fried in the frying pan with a little extra oil added.

6 Arrange the sausages, bacon, egg, fried bread (if using), tomato halves and mushrooms on a large hot platter and serve at once.

ACCOMPANIMENT
A 'full English' sometimes includes black or white pudding and often includes baked beans. To complete the breakfast, freshly made toast served with butter and marmalade is traditional.

PORRIDGE

North of the border porridge is taken seriously, and is still made in the traditional Scottish way – the oats cooked in water and stirred with a 'spurtle' stick. Although porridge oats are often used to make the more modern muesli, there is nothing like a bowl of the real thing to set you up on a cold day. And you don't have to be a purist – a puddle of cream, sprinkling of dark brown sugar or drizzle of golden honey can turn this healthy, quick-to-prepare food into something irresistible.

SERVES 1

INGREDIENTS
300 ml/10 fl oz water
40 g/1½ oz coarse oats
salt

1 Heat the water in a saucepan until boiling and pour in the oats, stirring continuously.

2 Allow to return to the boil and continue to stir for 2–3 minutes (or according to the packet instructions).

3 Add salt to taste and serve at once in a warm bowl.

ACCOMPANIMENT
In Scotland, porridge is traditionally served very simply as above, but many people prefer their porridge to be sweet. Serve with muscovado sugar, honey or golden syrup. The addition of milk is also more usual south of the border – you can make the porridge using all milk or half milk and half water, and serve with a helping of pouring cream on top. Some people like a grating of nutmeg, or a 'wee dram' can be poured over for a special occasion like New Year's Day. For a delicious and healthy option, serve your porridge with some fresh fruit, such as peaches or blueberries.

BRILLIANT BACON BUTTIE

Whether it is a quick breakfast to get you fuelled up in the morning or a late-night snack to help absorb the evening's alcohol, a bacon buttie certainly takes a lot of beating. It may not be the fanciest food, but the bacon buttie arouses some strong opinions. Should the bread be left plain, grilled or fried? White or wholemeal? To sauce or not to sauce? The only general consensus seems to be that the bread must be thick and it must be spread with a lot of butter.

SERVES 1

INGREDIENTS
2 smoked bacon rashers
15 g/½ oz butter, softened
2 slices thick white or brown
　bread
1 tomato, sliced (optional)
sauce of choice (brown sauce,
　tomato ketchup or mustard)
pepper

1 Cut the rashers of bacon in half so that you have 2 pieces of back bacon and 2 pieces of streaky.

2 Place the bacon under a hot grill and grill, turning frequently, until the bacon is cooked and as crispy as you like it.

3 Meanwhile, butter the bread.

4 Place 2 pieces of bacon on one slice of bread and season with a grinding of pepper. Add the tomato, if using, and the sauce. Top with the remaining bacon and the other slice of bread and eat immediately.

VARIATIONS
Toasted Sarnies
Make as above but toast the bread on both sides either under a medium grill or in a toaster before making the sandwich.

SMASHING SAUSAGE SANDWICH

After a late night out, nothing beats a sausage sandwich for settling the stomach and filling the hunger gap. Britain is a nation of sausage lovers and there are many different variations on the great British banger available – from delicately flavoured versions seasoned with herbs and maybe a touch of black pepper to more exotic creations spiked with chilli and other spices. Experiment with a few different kinds and choose your favourite to make this sandwich.

SERVES 1

INGREDIENTS

3 good-quality pork sausages
15 g/½ oz butter, softened
2 slices thick white or brown
    bread
sauce of choice (brown sauce,
    tomato ketchup or mustard)
pepper

1 Place the sausages under a hot grill and grill for 15–20 minutes, turning frequently, until they are well browned.

2 Meanwhile, butter the bread.

3 Place the sausages on one slice of bread and season with a grinding of pepper. Add the sauce and top with the other slice of bread. Eat immediately.

EGGS are for many people the number one comfort food, and if your happiest childhood memories include boiled eggs and soldiers, you're probably one of them. Eggs are very quick to prepare and nutritious, and can be cooked in so many different ways, from boiling and frying to scrambling, poaching and baking, that you don't have to keep them just for breakfast. A really fresh omelette cooked with a handful of fresh herbs or a filling makes one of the most elegant of all light lunch or supper dishes.

WAYS WITH EGGS

BOILING

You will need a saucepan large enough to cook the number of eggs required, but not so large that the eggs can move around too freely and crack. It is a good idea to have the eggs at room temperature to prevent cracking. Bring the water to a gentle simmer and lower the eggs in using a long-handled spoon. Simmer for 3–4 minutes for soft-boiled, 5–6 for medium-boiled and 10 minutes for hard-boiled. If you are serving hard-boiled eggs cold, always run them under cold water immediately after they are cooked to prevent a black line forming around the yolk.

SCRAMBLING

Allow 2 eggs per person and beat them gently in a basin with a little salt and pepper. Melt 15 g/½ oz butter in a saucepan over a low heat, pour in the beaten eggs and stir gently using a wooden spoon. The egg will start to set on the base of the pan, so lift it away from the base until all the egg is starting to look creamy. Remove from the heat and continue to stir until it does not look wet any more. Serve quickly as you do not want to have rubbery scrambled eggs.

POACHING

You need a small shallow pan (a small frying pan is ideal) and really fresh eggs for this method. Heat enough water to cover the eggs and break 1 egg into a cup. When the water is at a gentle simmer, carefully pour in the egg and allow the white to coagulate around the yolk. You can now add a further egg (I think 2 cooked together are enough to handle). Poach for 2–3 minutes if you like a soft yolk or for 4–5 minutes for a firmer egg. Remove from the pan using a slotted spoon, drain quickly on kitchen paper and serve immediately.

BAKING

If you have a large number of people to feed, baked eggs are a simple and delicious way to serve them. Generously butter a number of small ramekins and break 1 egg into each dish. Season well with salt and pepper and spoon over 1 tablespoon single cream. Place the dishes in a roasting tin with enough hot water to come halfway up the sides of the dishes and bake at 190°C/375°F/Gas Mark 5 for 15 minutes for a soft egg and 18–20 minutes for a firmer egg.

FRYING

The best way to fry an egg is in the same frying pan in which you have just fried some bacon. This way you have the delicious bacon fat to baste your egg with. Otherwise, take 1 tablespoon oil or 15 g/½ oz butter and heat in a small frying pan over a medium heat. Break the egg into the frying pan (if you are a beginner it might be wise to break the egg into a cup or ramekin first).

Fry for a few seconds until the white sets, then baste with the fat to make sure it is evenly cooked with the white completely set and the yolk still remaining soft in the centre. Remove the egg from the pan using a wooden spatula and allow it to rest on a piece of kitchen paper for a second to absorb any excess fat. Serve immediately.

POTATO CAKES

Potato cakes used to be another way of using up leftover potatoes, but it is worth making some freshly mashed potato especially for this recipe because the cakes are particularly light and delicious when the mash is hot. These cakes are a cross between a drop scone and a scone and are a wonderful treat eaten at breakfast with bacon and eggs. They are also good for afternoon tea hot from the griddle. I can remember as a child enjoying these potato cakes with the butter dripping from them.

SERVES 8–10

INGREDIENTS
550 g/1 lb 4 oz floury potatoes, such as King Edwards, Maris Piper or Desirée, peeled and cut into chunks
25 g/1 oz butter, plus extra to serve
1 egg (optional)
115 g/4 oz plain flour
salt and pepper

1 To make the mashed potato, cook the potatoes in a large saucepan of boiling salted water for 15–20 minutes. Drain well and mash with a potato masher until smooth. Season with salt and pepper and add the butter. Mix in the egg, if using.

2 Turn the mixture out into a large mixing bowl and add enough of the flour to make a light dough. Work quickly as you do not want the potato to cool too much.

3 Place the dough on a lightly floured surface and roll out carefully to a thickness of 5 mm/¼ inch. Using a 6-cm/2½-inch pastry cutter, cut into potato cakes.

4 Heat a greased griddle or heavy-based frying pan. Slip the cakes onto the griddle in batches and cook for 4–5 minutes on each side until they are golden brown.

5 Keep warm on a hot plate and serve immediately with lots of fresh butter.

VARIATION
For a more substantial supper dish for 3–4 people, you could make the potato cakes with a little chopped bacon and sautéed onion. Make the cakes thicker and fry in a mixture of oil and butter for 3–4 minutes on each side. Turn only once to avoid breaking the cakes. Serve hot with a green salad.

KEDGEREE

This Anglo-Indian dish of curried rice and fish was brought back to Britain in the time of the Raj by those who had developed a love of curry in their years abroad and couldn't wait to spice up the bland food of home. It was traditionally served as part of a breakfast buffet so that guests could help themselves from the sideboard, and today it makes a good dish to serve at brunch. Invite some friends over to chat and read the papers and serve Buck's Fizz to make the party really sparkle.

SERVES 4

INGREDIENTS
450 g/1 lb undyed smoked
   haddock, skinned
2 tbsp olive oil
1 onion, finely chopped
1 tsp mild curry paste
175 g/6 oz long-grain rice
55 g/2 oz butter
3 hard-boiled eggs
salt and pepper
2 tbsp chopped fresh parsley,
   to garnish

1 Place the fish in a large saucepan and cover with water. Bring the water to the boil, then turn down to a simmer and poach the fish for 8–10 minutes until it flakes easily.

2 Remove the fish and keep warm, reserving the water in a jug or bowl.

3 Add the oil to the saucepan and gently soften the onion for about 4 minutes. Stir in the curry paste and add the rice.

4 Measure 600 ml/1 pint of the haddock water and return to the saucepan. Bring to a simmer and cover. Cook for 10–12 minutes until the rice is tender and the water has been absorbed. Season to taste with salt and pepper.

5 Flake the fish and add to the saucepan with the butter. Stir very gently over a low heat until the butter has melted. Chop 2 of the hard-boiled eggs and add to the saucepan.

6 Turn the kedgeree into a serving dish, slice the remaining egg and use to garnish. Scatter the parsley over and serve at once.

VARIATION
Kedgeree can also be made with salmon and served as a lunch or supper dish.

KIPPERS

Kippers are herrings that have been split open, soaked in brine and then smoked over oak chips. They have a strong smoky flavour and can be quite salty, but make a delicious breakfast. The favoured food of the old-fashioned seaside hotel, kippers come from Scotland and the Isle of Man. Kippers can be grilled, fried or poached, but poaching has the advantage of keeping the fish moist and it also reduces the kipper smell during cooking.

SERVES 1

INGREDIENTS
1 kipper
knob of butter
pepper
buttered brown bread and lemon
   wedges, to serve

1 Place the kipper in a frying pan and cover with water.

2 Bring to the boil, then reduce the heat, cover and simmer gently for about 5 minutes.

3 Drain on kitchen paper and place on a warm plate with a knob of butter on top and some pepper to taste.

4 Serve immediately with the buttered brown bread and a squeeze of lemon juice.

ACCOMPANIMENT
Kippers are delicious served with a poached egg on top. They also make a delicious pâté, blended with softened butter and lemon juice.

WELSH RAREBIT

Toast is a great snack, whether buttered or topped with Marmite, honey or jam, and something on toast is always good for breakfast. The simplest is obviously baked beans, but some old favourites like Welsh rarebit remain very popular. There were English, Scottish and Welsh varieties as early as the eighteenth century, but the Welsh version is the one that seems to have lasted longest. Traditionally it was made with Welsh cheese, but it is now made with any well-flavoured Cheddar.

SERVES 4

INGREDIENTS
4 slices thick white or brown
   bread
225 g/8 oz mature Cheddar
   cheese, grated
25 g/1 oz butter
3 tbsp beer
½ tsp dry mustard powder
1 egg, beaten
salt and pepper

1 Toast the bread under a medium grill on 1 side only.

2 Put the cheese into a saucepan and add the butter and beer. Heat slowly over a low heat, stirring continuously. Add some salt and pepper and the mustard powder and stir well until the mixture is thick and creamy. Remove from the heat and allow to cool slightly before mixing in the egg.

3 Spread the rarebit over the untoasted side of the bread and place under the hot grill until golden and bubbling. Serve at once.

VARIATION
Scotch Woodcock
Toast 4 slices of granary or oat bread on both sides. Butter the slices and divide 12 anchovy fillets among them, keeping them warm. Melt 25 g/1 oz butter in a saucepan, add 6 beaten eggs and 2 tablespoons double cream. Season with salt, pepper and a pinch of cayenne pepper. Stir over a low heat, until the eggs are softly scrambled but still moist. Spoon the eggs over the anchovy toasts and serve with a sprinkling of snipped fresh chives. Serves 4.

2 SOUPS & STARTERS

Nothing sets the tone of the meal like your choice of starter, and soup is always a good option to wake up the taste buds. To the Scots, for example, a meal isn't complete without a bowl of soup, and you'll find a selection of British favourites in this chapter, from light Watercress Soup to spicy Mulligatawny Soup. Other unmistakably British starters include Potted Crab and Coronation Chicken, originally devised by chefs to serve at Queen Elizabeth II's coronation lunch. With dried fruit and a lightly curried sauce, this creamy dish has never fallen from favour. As a bonus, most of these recipes require nothing more than good bread to transform them into a satisfying lunch.

WATERCRESS SOUP

Watercress is extremely rich in vitamins and iron. With their peppery flavour, the leaves are fantastic stuffed into a grilled chicken and aïoli sandwich or a roast beef and horseradish roll. As well as making a great salad, it is wonderful cooked. In this recipe the watercress is used like baby spinach – the leaves are added at the last minute to conserve all the flavour, goodness and colour. The addition of crème fraîche gives this classic vegetable soup a fresh modern taste.

SERVES 4

INGREDIENTS
2 bunches watercress, thoroughly cleaned
40 g/1½ oz butter
2 onions, chopped
225 g/8 oz potatoes, peeled and roughly chopped
1.2 litres/2 pints vegetable stock or water
whole nutmeg, for grating
salt and pepper
crème fraîche and olive oil, to serve

1 Remove the leaves from the stalks of the watercress and keep on one side. Roughly chop the stalks.

2 Melt the butter in a large saucepan over a medium heat, add the onions and cook for 4–5 minutes until soft. Do not brown.

3 Add the potato to the saucepan and mix well with the onion. Add the watercress stalks and the stock.

4 Bring to the boil, then reduce the heat, cover and simmer for 15–20 minutes until the potato is soft.

5 Add the watercress leaves and stir in to heat through. Remove from the heat and use a hand-held stick blender to process the soup until smooth. Alternatively, liquidize the soup in a blender and return to the rinsed-out saucepan. Reheat and season with salt and pepper to taste, adding a good grating of nutmeg, if using.

6 Serve in warm bowls topped with a spoonful of crème fraîche, an extra grating of nutmeg and a drizzle of olive oil.

LEEK & POTATO SOUP

Leeks and potatoes are two of the staple vegetables of Britain and leeks are particularly associated with Wales, even appearing as one of the Welsh emblems. For cooking, small, tender leeks are better than the huge ones. This soup can be roughly blended to give a hearty, country texture or blended until smooth and served with cream and snipped chives for a more luxurious soup. When served cold, leek and potato soup is known as 'Vichyssoise'.

SERVES 4–6

INGREDIENTS
55 g/2 oz butter
1 onion, chopped
3 leeks, sliced
225 g/8 oz potatoes, peeled and
    cut into 2-cm/¾-inch cubes
850 ml/1½ pints vegetable stock
salt and pepper

TO GARNISH
150 ml/5 fl oz single cream
    (optional)
2 tbsp snipped fresh chives

1 Melt the butter in a large saucepan over a medium heat, add the prepared vegetables and sauté gently for 2–3 minutes until soft but not brown. Pour in the stock, bring to the boil, then reduce the heat and simmer, covered, for 15 minutes.

2 Remove from the heat and liquidize the soup in the saucepan using a hand-held stick blender if you have one. Otherwise, pour into a blender, liquidize until smooth and return to the rinsed-out saucepan.

3 Heat the soup, season with salt and pepper to taste and serve in warm bowls, swirled with the cream, if using, and garnished with chives.

COCK-A-LEEKIE SOUP

This Scottish soup is simply made with a whole chicken and leeks. Because the chicken is poached in the water, the resulting broth is highly flavoured. Some think the soup is better without the inclusion of prunes, which may date from medieval times, but they give this soup its uniqueness. This is a main course, more like a stew, and as it is not blended it is quite rustic. By discarding the slow-cooked vegetables and adding fresh leeks, this soup takes on a fresh flavour and colour.

SERVES 6–8

INGREDIENTS

2 tbsp vegetable cr olive oil
2 onions, roughly chopped
2 carrots, roughly chopped
5 leeks, 2 roughly chopped,
   3 thinly sliced
1 chicken, weighing 1.3 kg/3 lb
2 bay leaves
6 prunes, sliced
salt and pepper
sprigs of fresh parsley,
   to garnish

1 Heat the oil in a large saucepan over a medium heat, and then add the onions, carrots and 2 roughly chopped leeks. Sauté for 3–4 minutes until just golden brown.

2 Wipe the chicken inside and out and remove any excess skin and fat.

3 Place the chicken in the saucepan with the cooked vegetables and add the bay leaves. Pour in enough cold water to just cover and season well with salt and pepper. Bring to the boil, reduce the heat, then cover and simmer for 1–1½ hours. Skim off any scum that forms from time to time.

4 Remove the chicken from the stock, skin, then remove all the meat. Cut the meat into neat pieces.

5 Drain the stock through a colander, discard the vegetables and bay leaves and return to the rinsed-out saucepan. Expect to have 1.2–1.4 litres/2–2½ pints of stock. If you have time, it is a good idea to allow the stock to cool so that the fat may be removed. If not, blot the fat off the surface with pieces of kitchen paper.

6 Heat the stock to simmering point, add the sliced leeks and prunes to the saucepan and heat for about 1 minute.

7 Return the chicken to the pan and heat through. Serve immediately in warm deep dishes garnished with the parsley.

SCOTCH BROTH

Scotch broth is a very nourishing, hearty winter soup that is actually a meal in itself as it contains lamb, lots of vegetables and pearl barley. This is one of those 'one-pot' dishes that used to be served as a soup when people did more manual work, but today it is probably better served as a main course. Because lamb is quite a fatty meat, it is a good idea to make this soup the day before it is needed so that you can cool it and remove any excess fat.

SERVES 6–8

INGREDIENTS
700 g/1 lb 9 oz neck of lamb
1.7 litres/3 pints water
55 g/2 oz pearl barley
2 onions, chopped
1 garlic clove, finely chopped
3 small turnips, cut into small dice
3 carrots, peeled and finely sliced
2 celery sticks, sliced
2 leeks, sliced
salt and pepper
2 tbsp chopped fresh parsley, to garnish

1 Cut the meat into small pieces, removing as much fat as possible. Put into a large saucepan and cover with the water. Bring to the boil over a medium heat and skim off any scum that appears.

2 Add the pearl barley, reduce the heat and cook gently, covered, for 1 hour.

3 Add the prepared vegetables and season well with salt and pepper. Continue to cook for a further hour. Remove from the heat and allow to cool slightly.

4 Remove the meat from the saucepan using a slotted spoon and strip the meat from the bones. Discard the bones and any fat or gristle. Place the meat back in the saucepan and leave to cool thoroughly, then refrigerate overnight.

5 Scrape the solidified fat off the surface of the soup. Reheat, season with salt and pepper to taste and serve piping hot, garnished with the parsley scattered over the top.

MULLIGATAWNY SOUP

Mulligatawny soup is another Anglo-Indian dish flavoured with curry. The name 'Mulligatawny' comes from the Indian term for 'pepper water', which refers to the basic stock used. The wives of serving officers brought recipes from India back to Britain, where they became very popular long before the Indian take-away. The addition of apple is very good as the fruit complements the curry flavour, while the chopped coriander adds an authentic Indian taste.

SERVES 4–6

INGREDIENTS
55 g/2 oz butter
2 onions, chopped
1 small turnip, cut into small dice
2 carrots, sliced finely
1 Cox's apple, cored, peeled and chopped
2 tbsp mild curry powder
1.2 litres/2 pints chicken stock
juice of ½ lemon
175 g/6 oz cold cooked chicken, cut into small pieces
2 tbsp chopped fresh coriander
salt and pepper
55 g/2 oz cooked rice, to serve

1 Melt the butter in a large saucepan over a medium heat, add the onions and sauté gently until soft but not brown.

2 Add the prepared vegetables and apple and continue to cook for a further few minutes.

3 Stir in the curry powder until the vegetables are well coated, then pour in the stock. Bring to the boil, cover and simmer for about 45 minutes. Season well with salt and pepper to taste and add the lemon juice.

4 Liquidize the soup with a hand-held stick blender in the saucepan. Alternatively, pour into a blender, liquidize until smooth and return to the rinsed-out saucepan. Add the chicken and coriander to the saucepan and heat through.

5 Serve in warm bowls with a spoonful of the rice in the base and the soup poured over the top.

VARIATION
This soup is good served cold in summer with extra apple and a tablespoon of mango chutney.

JERUSALEM ARTICHOKE SOUP

Jerusalem artichokes are not related to the globe artichoke, and they do not come from Jerusalem. These knobbly root vegetables are a relation of the sunflower, and 'girasol', an old word for sunflower, was altered to 'Jerusalem'. For years they were not popular as they were difficult to peel, but there are newer varieties that are less knobbly and much easier to peel. The flavour is nutty and the texture produces a very creamy soup without the addition of cream.

SERVES 4–6

INGREDIENTS
55 g/2 oz butter
2 onions, chopped
675 g/1 lb 8 oz Jerusalem
    artichokes, peeled and sliced
850 ml/1½ pints chicken or
    vegetable stock
300 ml/10 fl oz milk
salt and pepper

CROÛTONS
2 slices day-old white bread,
    crusts removed
4 tbsp vegetable oil

1 To make the croûtons, cut the bread into 1-cm/½-inch cubes. Heat the oil in a frying pan and fry the croûtons in a single layer, tossing occasionally, until they are golden brown and crisp. Remove the pan from the heat and spoon out the croûtons onto kitchen paper to drain. Use on the day of making.

2 Melt the butter in a large saucepan over a medium heat, add the onions and cook until soft.

3 Add the Jerusalem artichokes and mix well with the butter, cover the saucepan and sauté slowly over a low heat for about 10 minutes. Pour in the stock, bring to the boil, then reduce the heat and simmer, covered, for 20 minutes.

4 Remove from the heat and liquidize the soup in the saucepan using a hand-held stick blender if you have one. Otherwise, pour into a blender, liquidize until smooth and return to the rinsed-out saucepan. Stir in the milk and season with salt and pepper to taste.

5 Heat the soup until hot and serve with the crispy croûtons.

VARIATION
A luxury addition to this soup is to slice 4–6 fresh scallops and poach for 2–3 minutes in the finished soup until cooked through.

PRAWN COCKTAIL

Of all the starters served in Britain, only the prawn cocktail has managed to achieve food icon status. It became popular as post-war austerity was replaced by restaurant dining, which for many meant a prawn cocktail followed by steak and chips. It has recently emerged from an unfashionable phase to find new popularity. The dressing can be created from home-made or bought mayonnaise and flavoured with spicy and tangy additions.

SERVES 4

INGREDIENTS
½ iceberg lettuce, finely
  shredded
150 ml/5 fl oz mayonnaise
2 tbsp single cream
2 tbsp tomato ketchup
few drops of Tabasco sauce
juice of ½ lemon
175 g/6 oz cooked peeled
  prawns
salt and pepper

TO GARNISH/SERVE
pinch of ground paprika
4 cooked prawns in their shells
4 lemon wedges
buttered brown bread

1 Divide the lettuce between 4 small serving dishes (traditionally, stemmed glass ones, but any small dishes will be fine).

2 Mix together the mayonnaise, cream and tomato ketchup in a bowl. Add Tabasco and lemon juice to your taste and season well with salt and pepper.

3 Divide the peeled prawns equally between the dishes and pour over the dressing. Chill for 30 minutes in the refrigerator.

4 Sprinkle a little paprika over the cocktails and garnish with a prawn and a lemon wedge on each dish. Serve with the buttered brown bread.

VARIATIONS
Other fish cocktails can be made in the same way. Try using crabmeat, lobster or a mixture of seafood. A more modern approach is to serve the prawns with avocado or mango and to add lime juice and fish sauce as flavourings, omitting the mayonnaise.

CHICKEN LIVER PÂTÉ

Pâtés have been around for centuries and are a good way to stretch small quantities of meat or fish. Early versions were very often coarsely made by roughly chopping up the meat with seasonings and added fat. The advent of mechanical mincers and electric mixers resulted in rich, silky-smooth pâtés which are often served in small quantities as starters. Pâté is ideal as a lunch or supper dish with lots of hot buttered toast or chunks of bread.

SERVES 4

INGREDIENTS
140 g/5 oz butter
1 onion, finely chopped
1 garlic clove, finely chopped
250 g/9 oz chicken livers
½ tsp Dijon mustard
2 tbsp brandy (optional)
salt and pepper
brown toast fingers, to serve

1 Melt half the butter in a large frying pan over a medium heat and cook the onion for 3–4 minutes until soft and transparent. Add the garlic and continue to cook for a further 2 minutes.

2 Check the chicken livers and remove any discoloured parts using a pair of scissors. Add the livers to the frying pan and cook over quite a high heat for 5–6 minutes until they are brown in colour.

3 Season well with salt and pepper and add the mustard and brandy, if using.

4 Process the pâté in a blender or food processor until smooth. Add the remaining butter cut into small pieces and process again until creamy.

5 Press the pâté into a serving dish or 4 small ramekins, smooth the surface and cover. If it is to be kept for more than 2 days, you could cover the surface with a little clarified butter (see page 66). Serve accompanied by toast fingers.

GARLIC MUSHROOMS

Savoury and simple, this rich and full-flavoured starter is ideal for entertaining, because it can be assembled up to a day in advance, ready for popping in the oven while you are enjoying drinks with friends. The only thing to worry about is that you have enough crusty bread to mop up all the buttery juices. Mushrooms come in many guises, and for this you want firm, large button or brown chestnut mushrooms that will hold the garlic and parsley stuffing.

SERVES 4

INGREDIENTS
450 g/1 lb button or chestnut
   mushrooms
175 g/6 oz softened butter
2 garlic cloves, crushed
juice and grated rind of ½ lemon
2 tbsp chopped fresh parsley
salt and pepper
fresh crusty bread, to serve

1 Preheat the oven to 220°C/425°F/Gas Mark 7. Remove the mushroom stalks and arrange the mushrooms, rounded-side down, in a shallow baking dish.

2 Mix the butter, garlic, lemon juice and rind, parsley, salt and pepper to taste together in a bowl. Divide the garlic butter between the mushroom cups.

3 Bake in the oven for 15–20 minutes, until the mushrooms are soft and the garlic butter is sizzling. Serve immediately with crusty bread.

CORONATION CHICKEN

Coronation chicken was devised for Queen Elizabeth II's Coronation lunch in June 1953 by Rosemary Hume and Constance Spry, co-principals of the Cordon Bleu cookery school. Since then it has become a great standby, often used for summer lunches and weddings. This recipe is made from chicken breasts, rather than a whole chicken, and the sauce includes apricots and yogurt. It is an ideal dish for a large number of guests (simply multiply the ingredients).

SERVES 6

INGREDIENTS
4 boneless chicken breasts
1 bay leaf
1 small onion, sliced
1 carrot, sliced
4 peppercorns
1 tbsp olive oil
2 shallots, finely chopped
2 tsp mild curry paste
2 tsp tomato purée
juice of ½ lemon
300 ml/10 fl oz mayonnaise
150 ml/5 fl oz natural yogurt
85 g/3 oz ready-to-eat dried
   apricots, chopped
salt and pepper
2 tbsp chopped fresh parsley,
   to garnish

1 Place the chicken breasts in a large saucepan with the bay leaf, onion and carrot. Cover with water and add ½ teaspoon salt and the peppercorns. Bring to the boil over a medium heat, reduce the heat and simmer very gently for 20–25 minutes. Remove from the heat and allow to cool in the liquor. Drain off 150 ml/5 fl oz of the stock for the sauce.

2 Meanwhile, heat the oil in a frying pan and sauté the shallots gently for 2–3 minutes until soft but not coloured. Stir in the curry paste and continue to cook for a further minute. Stir in the reserved stock, the tomato purée and the lemon juice and simmer for 10 minutes until the sauce is quite thick. Cool.

3 Remove the chicken from the stock, take off the skin and slice the meat into neat pieces.

4 Mix together the mayonnaise and the yogurt and stir into the sauce. Add the chopped apricots and season to taste with salt and pepper.

5 Stir the chicken into the sauce until well coated and turn into a serving dish. Allow to stand for at least 1 hour for the flavours to mingle. Serve garnished with the chopped parsley.

POTTED CRAB

'Potting' is a method from pre-refrigerator days for preserving all sorts of meat and fish. More recently, it became a way of stretching extravagant ingredients a little further. The food is packed into small pots and covered with a layer of butter or other solid fat to exclude the air. As a Lancashire lass, I remember eating potted shrimp from Morecambe Bay, turning out the pots to see the pale brown shrimp embedded in lovely yellow butter, then savouring every morsel.

SERVES 4–6

INGREDIENTS
1 large cooked crab, prepared by your fishmonger if possible
whole nutmeg, for grating
2 pinches of cayenne pepper or mace
juice of 1 lemon
225 g/8 oz lightly salted butter
salt and pepper
buttered toast, to serve

1 If the crab is not already prepared, pick out all the meat, taking great care to remove all the meat from the claws.

2 Mix together the white and brown meat but do not mash too smoothly. Season well with salt and pepper and add a good grating of nutmeg and the cayenne pepper. Add the lemon juice to taste.

3 Melt half the butter in a saucepan and carefully mix in the crabmeat. Turn the mixture out into 4–6 small soufflé dishes or ramekins.

4 In a clean saucepan, heat the remaining butter until it melts, then continue heating for a few moments until it stops bubbling. Allow the sediment to settle and carefully pour the clarified butter over the crab mixture. This seal of clarified butter allows the potted crab to be kept for 1–2 days. Chill in the refrigerator for 1–2 hours.

5 Serve with lots of buttered toast.

VARIATIONS
Shrimp, prawns, smoked salmon, smoked trout and smoked mackerel can also be potted in this way. As a great extravagance, lobster can be used.

3 ROASTS & PIES

A table graced with a roast joint of beef is an iconic image of traditional British cooking at its best. Although the traditional Sunday roast lunch might be less of a regular occurrence for most of us these days, a roast joint is ideal for family occasions and celebratory meals – Christmas just wouldn't be the same without a golden roasted turkey!

Savoury pies are one of Britain's contributions to global culinary traditions and are certainly worthy of the revival in popularity they are enjoying. Steak & Kidney Pie is a filling winter dish, while Pork & Apple Pie and Cornish Pasties are enjoyable year round and are great for picnics.

ROAST BEEF

Roast beef is probably the meal for which the British are known best around the world. Old paintings show the feasts of Tudor times, featuring huge ribs of beef served at Court – magnificent, and just how beef ought to be served. Roast beef is the most difficult roast to get right because, unlike other meats, you need to cook it so that it is still pink in the centre: careful timing is all. The best roast beef is a rib cooked on the bone, but this must be a good size.

SERVES 8

INGREDIENTS
2.7 kg/6 lb prime rib of beef
2 tsp dry English mustard
3 tbsp plain flour
300 ml/10 fl oz red wine
300 ml/10 fl oz beef stock
2 tsp Worcestershire sauce
  (optional)
salt and pepper
Yorkshire Pudding
  (see Accompaniment),
  to serve

1 Preheat the oven to 230°C/450°F/Gas Mark 8.

2 Season the meat with the salt and pepper and rub in the mustard and 1 tablespoon of the flour.

3 Place the meat in a roasting tin large enough to hold it comfortably and roast for 15 minutes. Reduce the heat to 190°C/375°F/Gas Mark 5 and cook for 15 minutes per 450 g/1 lb, plus 15 minutes (1 hour 45 minutes for this joint) for rare beef or 20 minutes per 450 g/1 lb, plus 20 minutes (2 hours 20 minutes) for medium beef. Baste the meat from time to time to keep it moist and if the tin becomes too dry, add a little stock or red wine.

4 Remove the meat from the oven and place on a hot serving plate, cover with foil and leave in a warm place for 10–15 minutes.

5 To make the gravy, pour off most of the fat from the tin (reserve it for the Yorkshire pudding), leaving behind the meat juices and the sediments. Place the tin on the top of the stove over a medium heat and scrape all the sediments from the base of the tin. Sprinkle in the remaining flour and quickly mix it into the juices with a small whisk. When you have a smooth paste, gradually add the wine and most of the stock, whisking all the time. Bring to the boil, then turn down the heat to a gentle simmer and cook for 2–3 minutes. Season with salt and pepper and add the remaining stock, if needed, and a little Worcestershire sauce, if liked.

6 When ready to serve, carve the meat into slices and serve on hot plates. Pour the gravy into a warm jug and take direct to the table. Serve with Yorkshire pudding.

ACCOMPANIMENT
Yorkshire Pudding
Preheat the oven to 220°C/425°F/ Gas Mark 7. Make a batter with 100 g/3½ oz plain flour, a pinch of salt, 1 beaten egg and 300 ml/ 10 fl oz milk and water mixed. Allow to stand for half an hour. Heat 2 tbsp roast beef dripping or olive oil in a 20-cm/8-inch square roasting tin in the top of the oven. Remove the tin from the oven, pour in the batter and bake for 25–30 minutes until it is puffed up and golden brown. Serves 4.

ROAST LEG OF LAMB

Rosemary and garlic have a natural affinity with lamb, and this traditional Sunday lunch dish fills the whole house with wonderful aromas as it roasts, invoking images of when it was a regular occurrence for families to sit down to a roast lunch every Sunday. A sharp redcurrant jelly and wine glaze adds sweetness and cuts through the richness of the meat. Leg is an excellent cut for roasting as the meat becomes meltingly tender and the pan juices make a flavoursome sauce.

SERVES 6

INGREDIENTS
1 leg of lamb, weighing 1.5 kg/
   3 lb 5 oz
6 garlic cloves, thinly sliced
   lengthways
8 fresh rosemary sprigs
salt and pepper
4 tbsp olive oil

GLAZE
4 tbsp redcurrant jelly
300 ml/10 fl oz rosé wine

1 Preheat the oven to 200°C/400°F/Gas Mark 6. Using a small knife, cut slits all over the leg of lamb. Insert 1–2 garlic slices and 4–5 rosemary needles in each slit. Place any remaining rosemary in the base of a roasting tin. Season the lamb to taste with salt and pepper and place in the roasting tin. Pour over the oil. Cover with foil and roast for 1 hour 20 minutes.

2 Mix the redcurrant jelly and wine together in a small saucepan. Heat gently, stirring constantly, until combined. Bring to the boil, then reduce the heat and simmer until reduced. Remove the lamb from the oven and pour over the glaze. Return to the oven and cook uncovered for about 10 minutes, depending on how well done you like it.

3 Remove the lamb from the roasting tin, cover with foil and leave to rest for 15 minutes before carving and serving.

ROAST PORK WITH CRACKLING

Roast pork can be delicious or disappointing. It is all to do with the quality of the pork and whether the fat will 'crackle' properly. The crackling is all important. It is the favourite part of the joint and unless it is crisp and crunchy the whole meal can be a disappointment. The best joints of pork for roasting are the leg and the loin. Choose the leg if you are catering for large numbers, although the loin, which can be bought in smaller sizes, is the best for crackling.

SERVES 4

INGREDIENTS
1 kg/2 lb 4 oz piece of pork loin, boned and the skin removed and reserved
2 tbsp mustard
salt and pepper
Apple Sauce (see Accompaniment), to serve

GRAVY
1 tbsp flour
300 ml/10 fl oz cider, apple juice or stock

1 Preheat the oven to 200°C/400°F/Gas Mark 6.

2 Make sure the skin of the pork is well scored and sprinkle with salt. Place on a wire rack on a baking tray and roast for 30–40 minutes until the crackling is golden brown and crispy. This can be cooked in advance, leaving room in the oven for roast potatoes.

3 Season the loin of pork well with salt and pepper and spread the fat with the mustard. Place in a roasting tin and roast in the centre of the oven for 20 minutes. Reduce the oven temperature to 190°C/375°F/Gas Mark 5 and cook for 50–60 minutes until the meat is a good colour and the juices run clear when the meat is pierced with a skewer.

4 Remove the meat from the oven and place on a hot serving plate, cover with foil and leave in a warm place.

5 To make the gravy, pour off most of the fat from the roasting tin, leaving the meat juices and the sediments. Sprinkle in the flour, whisking well. Cook the paste for a couple of minutes, then add the cider a little at a time until you have a smooth gravy. Boil for 2–3 minutes until it is the required consistency. Season well with salt and pepper and pour into a hot serving jug.

6 Carve the pork into slices and serve on hot plates with pieces of the crackling and the gravy. Serve with apple sauce.

ACCOMPANIMENT
Apple Sauce
Peel, core and slice 450 g/1 lb Bramley apples into a medium saucepan. Add 3 tablespoons water and 15 g/½ oz caster sugar and cook over a gentle heat for 10 minutes, stirring from time to time. A little ground cinnamon could be added, as could 15 g/ ½ oz butter, if desired. Beat well until the sauce is thick and smooth – use a hand mixer for a really smooth finish.

ROAST CHICKEN

Chicken has become a well-established favourite in recent years, though it was once seen as quite exclusive. Simply roasted, with lots of thyme and lemon, chicken produces a succulent gastronomic feast for many occasions. Try to buy a good fresh chicken as frozen birds do not have as much flavour. You can stuff your chicken with a traditional stuffing, such as sage and onion, or fruit, like apricots and prunes, but often the best way is to keep it simple.

SERVES 6

INGREDIENTS
2.25 kg/5 lb free-range chicken
55 g/2 oz butter
2 tbsp chopped fresh lemon
   thyme
1 lemon, quartered
125 ml/4 fl oz white wine
salt and pepper
6 sprigs of fresh thyme,
   to garnish

1 Preheat the oven to 220°C/425°F/ Gas Mark 7.

2 Make sure the chicken is clean, wiping it inside and out using kitchen paper, and place in a roasting tin.

3 In a bowl, soften the butter with a fork, mix in the herbs and season well with salt and pepper.

4 Butter the chicken all over with the herb butter, inside and out, and place the lemon pieces inside the body cavity. Pour the wine over the chicken.

5 Roast in the centre of the oven for 20 minutes. Reduce the temperature to 190°C/375°F/Gas Mark 5 and continue to roast for a further 1¼ hours, basting frequently. Cover with foil if the skin begins to brown too much. If the tin dries out, add a little more wine or water.

6 Test that the chicken is cooked by piercing the thickest part of the leg with a sharp knife or skewer and making sure the juices run clear. Remove from the oven.

7 Remove the chicken from the roasting tin, place on a warmed serving plate and leave to rest for 10 minutes before carving.

8 Place the roasting tin on the top of the stove and bubble the pan juices gently over a low heat until they have reduced and are thick and glossy. Season with salt and pepper to taste.

9 Serve the chicken with the pan juices and scatter with the thyme sprigs.

ROAST TURKEY WITH TWO STUFFINGS

Turkey is now the favourite Christmas dinner in Britain. Roast turkey, served with all the trimmings, is the seasonal favourite many of us look forward to. There is much debate as to whether it is safe to stuff the bird. On the following pages, I give a celery and walnut stuffing for the body that is not too dense and also keeps the bird moist, and offer an alternative traditional chestnut stuffing for the neck. One stuffing will suffice, but two are even better and add more variety to this delicious combination of flavours. Cocktail sausages and bacon rolls are often served with roast turkey, especially at Christmas. Brussels sprouts mixed with some chopped chestnuts are also traditional, as are roast potatoes and parsnips.

SERVES 4

INGREDIENTS
4.5 kg/10 lb turkey
115 g/4 oz butter, softened
10 streaky bacon rashers
salt and pepper

1 Preheat the oven to 220°C/425°F/Gas Mark 7.

2 Wipe the turkey inside and out with kitchen paper. Season, both inside and out, with salt and pepper.

3 Stuff the body cavity of the turkey with the celery and walnut stuffing and the neck with the chestnut stuffing (for recipes see overleaf). Secure the neck skin with metal skewers and the legs with string.

4 Cover the bird all over with the butter and squeeze some under the breast skin. Use a little to grease the roasting tin. Place the bird in the tin, season again with salt and pepper and cover the breast with the bacon rashers.

5 Cover the bird with foil and roast in the oven for 30 minutes. Reduce the oven temperature to 180°C/350°F/Gas Mark 4 and continue to cook for 2½–3 hours, basting the turkey every 30 minutes with the pan juices.

6 About 45 minutes before the end of the cooking time, remove the foil and allow the turkey to brown, basting from time to time. Remove the bacon rashers when crispy and keep warm.

7 Test that the turkey is cooked by piercing the thickest part of the leg with a sharp knife or skewer to make sure the juices run clear. Also, pull a leg slightly away from the body; it should feel loose.

8 Remove the turkey from the roasting tin and place on a warm serving plate, cover with foil and leave to rest whilst you complete the remainder of the meal. The turkey may be left to rest in this way for up to 1 hour before serving.

See over for accompaniments

ACCOMPANIMENTS

Roast turkey would not be the same without all the trimmings. Cranberry sauce and bread sauce are the traditional accompaniments and proper gravy, made with the juices from the roasting tin, is a real treat. Other favourite side dishes include Brussels sprouts mixed with some chopped chestnuts, and crispy roast potatoes and parsnips.

CELERY & WALNUT STUFFING

INGREDIENTS
2 onions, finely chopped
2 tbsp butter
55 g/2 oz fresh wholemeal
  breadcrumbs
4 celery sticks, chopped
2 Cox's apples, cored and
  roughly chopped
115 g/4 oz dried ready-to-eat
  apricots, chopped
115 g/4 oz walnuts, chopped
2 tbsp chopped fresh parsley
salt and pepper

1 Fry the onions in the butter in a frying pan until soft.
2 In a bowl, mix together the breadcrumbs, celery, apples, apricots and walnuts. Add the cooked onion and season to taste with salt and pepper. Stir in the parsley.
3 Cool before using to stuff the turkey.

CHESTNUT STUFFING

INGREDIENTS
115 g/4 oz lardons or strips of
  streaky bacon
1 onion, finely chopped
2 tbsp butter
115 g/4 oz button mushrooms,
  sliced
225 g/8 oz chestnut purée
2 tbsp chopped fresh parsley
grated rind of 2 lemons
salt and pepper

1 Cook the lardons and onion in the butter in a frying pan until soft. Add the mushrooms and cook for 1–2 minutes, then remove from the heat.
2 In a bowl, mix together the chestnut purée with the parsley and lemon rind and season well with salt and pepper. Add the contents of the frying pan to the bowl and mix well.
3 Cool before using to stuff the turkey.

GRAVY

INGREDIENTS
2 tbsp plain flour
1 litre/1¾ pints stock, if possible
  made from the giblets
125 ml/4 fl oz red wine or sherry

1 Remove the fat from the turkey roasting tin and place the tin over a low heat on top of the stove.
2 Sprinkle in the flour, stir well using a small whisk to make a smooth paste and cook for 1 minute. Add the stock a little at a time, whisking constantly, until you have a smooth gravy.
3 Add the wine and bubble together until the gravy is slightly reduced. Season to taste.
4 When you carve the turkey some meat juices will escape: add these to the gravy and stir. Carefully pour the gravy into a warm serving jug and serve with the turkey.

BREAD SAUCE

INGREDIENTS
1 onion, peeled but left whole
12 cloves
1 bay leaf
6 peppercorns
600 ml/1 pint milk
115 g/4 oz fresh white
   breadcrumbs
25 g/1 oz butter
½ tsp grated nutmeg
2 tbsp double cream (optional)
salt and pepper

1 Make 12 small holes in the onion using a skewer and stick a clove in each hole.
2 Place the onion, bay leaf and peppercorns in a small saucepan and pour in the milk. Place over a medium heat, bring to the boil, remove from the heat, then cover and leave to infuse for 1 hour.
3 Strain the milk and discard the onion, bay leaf and peppercorns.
4 Return the milk to the rinsed-out saucepan and add the breadcrumbs. Cook the sauce over a very gentle heat until the breadcrumbs have swollen and the sauce is thick. Beat in the butter and season well with salt and pepper to taste.
5 When ready to serve, reheat the sauce briefly, if necessary. Add the nutmeg and stir in the double cream, if using. Pour into a warm serving bowl and serve with the turkey.

CRANBERRY SAUCE

INGREDIENTS
225 g/8 oz fresh cranberries
85 g/3 oz soft brown sugar
150 ml/5 fl oz orange juice
½ tsp ground cinnamon
½ tsp grated nutmeg

1 Place the cranberries in a saucepan and add the sugar, orange juice, cinnamon and nutmeg.
2 Bring to the boil slowly, stirring from time to time. Cook for 8–10 minutes until the cranberries have burst, taking care as they may splash.
3 Put the sauce in a serving bowl and cover until needed. Serve warm or cold with the turkey.

BONED & STUFFED ROAST DUCK

Duck is wonderful to serve on a special occasion, the only drawback being that there is not much meat on the bird and it can be difficult to carve. Why not have your butcher bone the duck for you and then stuff it with good-quality sausage meat? I also add a couple of duck breasts to make a very substantial dish for 6–8 people that is easy to carve and looks wonderful. Serve with a sweet sauce: orange is classic, but I prefer to make one with canned apricots, spiced with cinnamon and ginger.

SERVES 6–8

INGREDIENTS
1.8 kg/4 lb duck (dressed weight), ask your butcher to bone the duck and cut off the wings at the first joint
450 g/1 lb flavoured sausage meat, such as pork and apricot
1 small onion, finely chopped
1 Cox's apple, cored and finely chopped
85 g/3 oz ready-to-eat dried apricots, finely chopped
85 g/3 oz chopped walnuts
2 tbsp chopped fresh parsley
1 large or 2 smaller duck breasts, skin removed
salt and pepper
Apricot Sauce (see Accompaniment), to serve

ACCOMPANIMENT
Apricot Sauce
Purée 400 g/14 oz canned apricot halves in syrup in a blender. Pour the purée into a saucepan and add 150 ml/5 fl oz stock, 125 ml/4 fl oz Marsala, ½ teaspoon ground cinnamon and ½ teaspoon ground ginger and season with salt and pepper. Stir over a low heat, then simmer for 2–3 minutes. Serve warm.

1 Wipe the duck with kitchen paper both inside and out. Lay it skin-side down on a board and season well with salt and pepper.

2 Mix together the sausage meat, onion, apple, apricots, walnuts and parsley and season well with salt and pepper. Form into a large sausage shape.

3 Lay the duck breast(s) on the whole duck and cover with the stuffing. Wrap the whole duck around the filling and tuck in any leg and neck flaps.

4 Preheat the oven to 190°C/375°F/Gas Mark 5.

5 Sew the duck up the back and across both ends with fine string. Try to use one piece of string so that you can remove it in one go. Mould the duck into a good shape and place, sewn-side down, on a wire rack over a roasting tin.

6 Roast for 1½–2 hours, basting occasionally. When it is cooked, the duck should be golden brown and crispy.

7 Carve the duck into thick slices at the table and serve with apricot sauce.

ROAST GAMMON

Roast gammon or ham has long been a favourite choice for Sunday lunch and for Boxing Day dinner. Both gammon and ham are salted, either by salt curing or soaking in brine, and some varieties, like York ham, can be smoked. Some joints may need to be soaked in water for 2 hours or overnight to reduce the saltiness (check with your butcher or on the packaging). The sweet glaze of hams, or the serving of a sweet accompaniment like Cumberland sauce, is to counteract the salt.

SERVES 6

INGREDIENTS

1.3 kg/3 lb boneless gammon,
   pre-soaked if necessary
2 tbsp Dijon mustard
85 g/3 oz demerara sugar
½ tsp ground cinnamon
½ tsp ground ginger
18 whole cloves
Cumberland Sauce
   (see Accompaniment),
   to serve

1 Place the joint in a large saucepan, cover with cold water and slowly bring to the boil over a gentle heat. Cover and simmer very gently for 1 hour.

2 Preheat the oven to 200°C/400°F/Gas Mark 6.

3 Remove the gammon from the pan and drain. Remove the rind from the gammon and discard. Score the fat into a diamond-shaped pattern with a sharp knife.

4 Spread the mustard over the fat. Mix together the sugar and the spices on a plate and roll the gammon in it, pressing down well to coat evenly.

5 Stud the diamond shapes with cloves and place the joint in a roasting tin. Roast for 20 minutes until the glaze is a rich golden colour.

6 To serve hot, allow to stand for 20 minutes before carving. If the gammon is to be served cold, it can be cooked a day ahead. Serve with Cumberland sauce.

ACCOMPANIMENT
Cumberland Sauce
Using a lemon zester, remove the zest of 2 oranges (Seville, when in season, are the best). Place 4 tablespoons redcurrant jelly in a small saucepan with 4 tablespoons port and 1 teaspoon mustard and heat gently until the jelly is melted. Cut the oranges in half and squeeze the juice into the pan. Add the orange zest and season with salt and pepper to taste. Serve cold with gammon. The sauce can be kept in a screw-top jar in the refrigerator for up to 2 weeks.

LANCASHIRE CHEESE-STUFFED PORK FILLET

Pork fillet or tenderloin is the tenderest part of the pig. It is very lean and can be sliced and cooked as escalopes or, as here, stuffed and sliced before serving. You can choose any stuffing, but this one using Lancashire cheese is a favourite from my childhood. The use of cider is also traditional – the combination of apples with pork goes back to the time when pigs were kept in farm orchards and allowed to eat the windfall apples: perhaps the apple flavour was apparent in the meat.

SERVES 4

INGREDIENTS
2 pork fillets, weighing 350 g/
   12 oz each
2 thin slices cooked ham
   (or use Parma ham)
85 g/3 oz Lancashire cheese,
   crumbled
4 ready-to-eat prunes, cut in half
4 fresh sage leaves, chopped
25 g/1 oz butter
225 ml/8 fl oz cider or apple juice
1 tsp mild mustard
125 ml/4 fl oz single cream
salt and pepper

1 Preheat the oven to 190°C/375°F/Gas Mark 5.

2 Cut the fillets down the centre, but do not cut right through. Spread them open and flatten out. You can bash the fillets with a rolling pin to flatten them out more if you wish.

3 Season the fillets well with salt and pepper and place a piece of ham on each one. Crumble over the cheese and arrange the prunes on top. Sprinkle over the sage leaves.

4 Fold the fillets over into neat sausage shapes and secure with cocktail sticks or tie with string to make sure they keep their shape.

5 Place in a small roasting tin, dot with the butter and pour over the cider.

6 Cover with foil and cook in the oven for 40–45 minutes, removing the foil for the last 10 minutes.

7 Remove the tin from the oven and place the pork on a warm plate. Remove the cocktail sticks or string and allow the meat to rest for 10 minutes in a warm place.

8 Place the roasting tin on the stove over a medium heat and stir the juices well to mix. Add the mustard and bubble away until the sauce is quite thick. Stir in the cream and heat through.

9 Slice the pork and serve with the sauce.

STEAK & KIDNEY PIE

Like steak and kidney pudding, this dish also goes by the cockney rhyming slang name of 'Kate & Sydney', and is just as traditional throughout Britain. Some people use shortcrust pastry, but the richer puff pastry is better as it gives a really crisp crust while allowing the base of the pastry to absorb some of the gravy and hence have a better flavour. There are of course regional variations of steak and kidney pie and some cooks add mushrooms and oysters.

SERVES 4–6

INGREDIENTS
butter, for greasing
700 g/1 lb 9 oz braising steak, trimmed and cut into 4-cm/1½-inch pieces
3 lambs' kidneys, cored and cut into 2.5-cm/1-inch pieces
2 tbsp plain flour, plus extra for dusting
3 tbsp vegetable oil
1 onion, roughly chopped
1 garlic clove, finely chopped
125 ml/4 fl oz red wine
450 ml/16 fl oz stock
1 bay leaf
400 g/14 oz ready-made puff pastry
1 egg, beaten
salt and pepper

1 Preheat the oven to 160°C/325°F/Gas Mark 3. Grease a 1.2-litre/2-pint pie dish.

2 Put the prepared meat into a large plastic bag with the flour and salt and pepper and shake well until all the meat is well coated.

3 Heat the oil in a flameproof casserole over a high heat and brown the meat in batches. Remove from the casserole with a slotted spoon and keep warm. Fry the onion and garlic in the casserole for 2–3 minutes until softening.

4 Stir in the wine and scrape the base of the pan to release the sediment. Pour in the stock, stirring constantly, and bring to the boil. Bubble for 2–3 minutes. Add the bay leaf and return the meat to the casserole. Cover and cook in the centre of the oven for 1½–2 hours. Check the seasoning, then remove the bay leaf. Leave the meat to cool, preferably overnight, to develop the flavours.

5 Preheat the oven to 200°C/400°F/Gas Mark 6.

6 Roll out the pastry on a lightly floured work surface to about 7 cm/2¾ inches larger than the pie dish. Cut off a 3-cm/1¼-inch strip from the edge. Moisten the rim of the dish and press the pastry strip onto it. Place a pie funnel in the centre of the dish and spoon in the steak and kidney filling. Don't overfill, keeping any extra gravy to serve separately. Moisten the pastry collar with water and put on the pastry lid, taking care to fit it carefully around the pie funnel. Crimp the edges of the pastry firmly and glaze with the egg.

7 Place the pie on a tray towards the top of the oven for about 30 minutes. The pie should be golden brown and the filling bubbling hot; cover it with foil and reduce the temperature if the pastry is getting too brown.

PORK & APPLE PIE

Raised pies, with the crisp hot-crust pastry, are one of the jewels of the British culinary crown. This home-made version, stuffed with lean pork, apples, potatoes and lots of seasonings, is a world away from cheap commercial pies. Try it and you'll soon understand why pies were once a regular feature of shooting parties and picnics. This is particularly good to have on hand for weekends when you are catering for lots of people as it may be eaten hot or cold.

SERVES 8

INGREDIENTS

900 g/2 lb waxy potatoes, peeled and sliced
2 tbsp butter
2 tbsp vegetable oil
450 g/1 lb lean boneless pork, cubed
2 onions, sliced
4 garlic cloves, crushed
4 tbsp tomato purée
600 ml/1 pint stock
2 tbsp chopped fresh sage
2 eating apples, peeled, cored and sliced
1 egg, beaten
1 tsp gelatine
salt and pepper

PASTRY

675 g/1 lb 8 oz plain flour, plus extra for dusting
pinch of salt
4 tbsp butter
125 g/4½ oz lard
300 m/10 fl oz water

1 To make the filling, cook the potatoes in a saucepan of boiling water for 10 minutes. Drain and set aside. Melt the butter with the oil in a flameproof casserole over a medium-high heat. Add the pork and cook until browned all over.

2 Add the onions and garlic and cook, stirring frequently, for 5 minutes. Stir in the pork, stock and sage. Season to taste with salt and pepper. Reduce the heat, cover and simmer for 1½ hours. Drain the stock from the casserole and reserve. Leave the pork to cool.

3 Preheat the oven to 200°C/400°F/ Gas Mark 6. To make the pastry, sift the flour and salt into a bowl. Make a well in the centre. Melt the butter and lard in a saucepan with the water, then bring to the boil. Pour into the well and gradually mix into the flour to form a dough. Turn out onto a lightly floured surface and knead until smooth. Reserve a quarter of the dough and use the remainder to line the base and sides of a large pie tin or deep 20-cm/8-inch round loose-based cake tin.

4 Layer the pork, potatoes and apples in the base. Roll out the reserved pastry to make a lid. Dampen the edges and put the lid on top, sealing well. Brush with the beaten egg to glaze. Make a hole in the top. Bake in the preheated oven for 30 minutes, then reduce the temperature to 160°C/325°F/Gas Mark 3 and bake for a further 45 minutes. Dissolve the gelatine in the reserved stock and pour into the hole in the lid as the pie cools. Serve well chilled.

VARIATION
You can make individual pork pies using 11-cm/4-inch pie tins. Bake in a preheated oven at 180°C/350°F/Gas Mark 4 for 30–40 minutes, until the pastry is golden brown and the filling is cooked through. Makes about 8.

CORNISH PASTIES

Cornish pasties were made by women for their menfolk to take down the tin mines. The pastry shape was a convenient one to put in the pocket. Sometimes the pasties had meat at one end and fruit at the other to make a complete meal. The filling is a mixture of beef, onions, potato and swede (sometimes known as turnip in Cornwall). Today, they are still popular throughout the West Country and are particularly good eaten hot from the oven in winter after a long, exhausting walk.

SERVES 4

INGREDIENTS
250 g/9 oz chuck steak, trimmed and cut into 1-cm/½-inch dice
175 g/6 oz swede, peeled and cut into 1-cm/½-inch dice
350 g/12 oz potatoes, peeled and cut into 1-cm/½-inch dice
1 onion, finely chopped
1 egg, beaten
salt and pepper

SHORTCRUST PASTRY
450 g/1 lb plain flour, plus extra for dusting
pinch of salt
115 g/4 oz lard
115 g/4 oz butter
175 ml/6 fl oz cold water

1 To make the pastry, sift the flour and salt into a bowl and gently rub in the lard and butter until the mixture resembles breadcrumbs. Add the water, a spoonful at a time, and stir the mixture with a knife until it holds together.

2 Turn out onto a lightly floured surface and gently press together until smooth. Wrap in clingfilm and allow to chill for 1 hour.

3 Meanwhile, to prepare the filling, mix the meat and vegetables together and season well with salt and pepper.

4 Divide the pastry into 4 even-sized pieces and roll one out until just larger than the size of a 20-cm/8-inch plate. Place the plate on top of the pastry and cut round it to give a neat edge. Repeat with the other pieces.

5 Arrange the meat and vegetable mixture across the 4 rounds of pastry, making sure the filling goes to the edge.

6 Brush the edges of the pastry with water, then bring the edges up over the filling and press together to form a ridge. You can flute the edges of the pasties with your fingers or fold over the pastry to form a cord-like seal. Tuck in the ends.

7 Allow to chill for 1 hour, then glaze with the egg.

8 Preheat the oven to 190°C/375°F/Gas Mark 5.

9 Place on a greased baking tray and cook in the centre of the oven for 50–60 minutes. The pasties should be crisp and golden in colour. Cover with foil and reduce the temperature if the pastry is getting too brown.

4 STEWS & BAKES

You may think that slow-cooked stews are from a bygone age when family cooks had plenty of time to spend in the kitchen, but they are, in fact, perfect for today's busier lifestyles. The recipes in this chapter require little attention while cooking and can easily be made a day or two ahead and then reheated — ideal for no-hassle entertaining. Frugal housewives have always valued Irish Stew, Game Pie and Steak & Kidney Pudding as economical recipes to keep a whole family satisfied. You'll also find some pub favourites here that are great family recipes, such as Sausages & Mash with Onion Gravy, Toad in the Hole and Shepherd's Pie.

LANCASHIRE HOTPOT

'Hotpot' refers to the deep earthenware lidded dish in which it was traditionally cooked. It is a very convenient meal because all the ingredients are cooked in one pot – I use a large, shallow gratin dish or a deep roasting tin so that the potatoes crisp up. The first hotpots were made with mutton, but today they are made with lamb. Lancashire hotpot is similar to Irish stew and may have other vegetables added, although the traditional recipe has just onions and potatoes.

SERVES 4–6

INGREDIENTS

900 g/2 lb best end lamb chops
3 lambs' kidneys
55 g/2 oz butter
900 g/2 lb floury potatoes, such as King Edwards or Maris Piper, peeled and sliced
3 onions, halved and finely sliced
2 tsp fresh thyme leaves
1 tsp finely chopped fresh rosemary
600 ml/1 pint chicken stock
salt and pepper

1 Preheat the oven to 160°C/325°F/Gas Mark 3.

2 Trim the chops of any excess fat. Cut the kidneys in half, remove the core and cut into quarters. Season all the meat well with salt and pepper.

3 Butter a large, shallow ovenproof dish or deep roasting tin with half the butter and arrange a layer of potatoes in the bottom. Layer up the onions and meat, seasoning well with salt and pepper and sprinkling the herbs between each layer. Finish with a neat layer of overlapping potatoes.

4 Pour in most of the stock so that it covers the meat.

5 Melt the remaining butter and brush the top of the potato with it. Reserve any remaining butter. Cover with foil and cook in the oven for 2 hours.

6 Uncover the hotpot and brush the potatoes again with the melted butter.

7 Return the hotpot to the oven and cook for a further 30 minutes, allowing the potatoes to get brown and crisp. You may need to increase the temperature if not browning sufficiently, or pop under a hot grill. Serve the hotpot at the table, making sure that everyone gets a good helping of potatoes and the meat.

BEEF STEW WITH HERB DUMPLINGS

This satisfying dish is ideal for cold winter months. It is prepared by long slow cooking in a liquid to ensure that the meat is melt-in-the-mouth tender. Originally it made use of tougher, cheaper cuts of meat and, sadly, the poor ingredients gave 'stew' a bad name. Here though, the dish is made with quality ingredients and topped with old-fashioned herb dumplings. This is traditional rib-sticking food, guaranteed to satisfy the heartiest appetites.

SERVES 6

INGREDIENTS
3 tbsp olive oil
2 onions, finely sliced
2 garlic cloves, chopped
1 kg/2 lb 4 oz good-quality
    braising steak
2 tbsp plain flour
300 ml/10 fl oz beef stock
bouquet garni (bunch of mixed
    fresh herbs)
150 ml/5 fl oz red wine
salt and pepper
1 tbsp chopped fresh parsley,
    to garnish

HERB DUMPLINGS
115 g/4 oz self-raising flour, plus
    extra for shaping
55 g/2 oz suet
1 tsp mustard
1 tbsp chopped fresh parsley
1 tsp chopped fresh sage
4 tbsp cold water
salt and pepper

1 Preheat the oven to 150°C/300°F/Gas Mark 2.

2 Heat 1 tablespoon of the oil in a large frying pan and fry the onion and garlic until soft and brown. Remove from the pan using a slotted spoon and place in a large casserole dish.

3 Trim the meat and cut into thick strips. Using the remaining oil, fry the meat in the frying pan over a high heat, stirring well until it is brown all over.

4 Sprinkle in the flour and stir well to prevent lumps. Season well.

5 Over a medium heat, pour in the stock, stirring all the time to make a smooth sauce, then continue to heat until boiling.

6 Carefully turn the contents of the frying pan into the casserole dish. Add the bouquet garni and the wine. Cover and cook gently in the oven for 2–2½ hours.

7 Start making the dumplings 20 minutes before the stew is ready. Place the flour, suet, mustard, herbs and seasoning in a bowl and mix well. Just before adding the dumplings to the stew, add enough of the water to the mixture to form a firm but soft dough. Break the dough into 12 pieces and roll them into round dumplings (you might need some flour on your hands for this).

8 Remove the stew from the oven, check the seasoning, discard the bouquet garni and add the dumplings, pushing them down under the liquid. Cover and return the dish to the oven, continuing to cook for 15 minutes until the dumplings have doubled in size.

9 Serve piping hot with the parsley scattered over the top.

VENISON CASSEROLE

Venison is a very British meat and is particularly associated with Scotland. It was traditionally the meat from wild deer, the hunting season being from late June to January, but farmed venison is now available all year round. Today venison is being eaten more and more because it is a healthy meat owing to its relatively low fat and cholesterol content. It tends to be a dry meat, though, so it is best to casserole it to ensure it is tender.

SERVES 4–6

INGREDIENTS

3 tbsp olive oil
1 kg/2 lb 4 oz casserole venison, cut into 3-cm/1¼-inch cubes
2 onions, finely sliced
2 garlic cloves, chopped
2 tbsp plain flour
350 ml/12 fl oz beef or vegetable stock
125 ml/4 fl oz port or red wine
2 tbsp redcurrant jelly
6 crushed juniper berries
pinch of ground cinnamon
whole nutmeg, for grating
175 g/6 oz vacuum-packed chestnuts (optional)
salt and pepper

1 Preheat the oven to 150°C/300°F/Gas Mark 2.

2 Heat the oil in a large frying pan and brown the cubes of venison over a high heat. You may need to fry the meat in 2 or 3 batches – do not overcrowd the frying pan. Remove the venison using a slotted spoon and place in a large casserole dish.

3 Add the onions and garlic to the frying pan and fry until a good golden colour, then add to the meat. Sprinkle the meat in the casserole dish with the flour and turn to coat evenly.

4 Gradually add the stock to the frying pan, stir well and scrape up the sediment, then bring to the boil. Add to the casserole dish and stir well, ensuring that the meat is just covered.

5 Add the port, redcurrant jelly, juniper berries, cinnamon, a small grating of nutmeg and the chestnuts, if using. Season well with the salt and pepper, cover and cook gently in the centre of the oven for 2–2½ hours.

6 Remove from the oven and season with more salt and pepper if necessary. Serve immediately, piping hot.

COOK'S TIP

This casserole benefits from being made the day before to allow the flavours to develop. Reheat gently before serving. Ensure you cool the casserole as quickly as possible and store in the refrigerator or a cool larder overnight. Serve the casserole with baked or mashed potatoes.

IRISH STEW

This classic dish of lamb, potatoes and onions was traditionally a cheap way to fill up a hungry family, but now it is appreciated much more for its delicious flavours and is often featured on upmarket restaurant menus. Inexpensive middle neck of lamb, or mutton, is commonly used, along with potatoes and onions – this tasty recipe includes sliced carrots for extra flavour. You need a firm potato that will hold its shape during the long, gentle cooking. Maris Piper or Romano are ideal.

SERVES 4

INGREDIENTS
4 tbsp plain flour
1.3 kg/3 lb middle neck of lamb,
   trimmed of visible fat
3 large onions, chopped
3 carrots, sliced
450 g/1 lb potatoes, peeled and
   cut into wedges
½ tsp dried thyme
850 ml/1½ pints hot beef stock
salt and pepper
2 tbsp chopped fresh parsley,
   to garnish

1 Preheat the oven to 160°C/325°F/Gas Mark 3. Spread the flour on a plate and season with salt and pepper. Roll the pieces of lamb in the flour to coat, shaking off any excess, and arrange in the base of a casserole.

2 Layer the onions, carrots and potatoes on top of the lamb.

3 Sprinkle in the thyme and pour in the stock, then cover and cook in the preheated oven for 2½ hours. Garnish with the chopped fresh parsley and serve straight from the casserole.

ACCOMPANIMENT
For an authentic touch, serve this stew with fresh home-made Soda Bread (see page 215).

GAME PIE

Game is the term given to wild animals and birds that are hunted for the table. Today, however, many of these same animals are farmed or bred especially. The most popular birds are wild duck, pheasant, grouse, partridge, woodcock, pigeon and quail. Game animals include deer (venison), rabbit, hare and wild boar. For a pie, any meat or combination of meats can be used, although the cooking time will vary according to the type and cut of meat.

SERVES 4–6

INGREDIENTS
oil, for greasing
700 g/1 lb 9 oz mixed game, cut into 3-cm/1¼-inch pieces
2 tbsp plain flour, plus extra for dusting
3 tbsp vegetable oil
1 onion, roughly chopped
1 garlic clove, finely chopped
350 g/12 oz large field mushrooms, sliced
1 tsp crushed juniper berries
125 ml/4 fl oz port or Marsala
450 ml/16 fl oz chicken or game stock
1 bay leaf
400 g/14 oz ready-made puff pastry
1 egg, beaten
salt and pepper

1 Preheat the oven to 160°C/325°F/Gas Mark 3. Grease a 1.2-litre/2-pint pie dish. Put the meat into a large plastic bag with the flour and salt and pepper and shake to coat the meat.

2 Heat the oil in a large flameproof casserole dish over a high heat and brown the meat in batches. Remove with a slotted spoon and keep warm. Fry the onion and garlic for 2–3 minutes until softened, then add the mushrooms and cook for about 2 minutes, stirring constantly, until they start to wilt. Add the juniper berries, then the port and scrape the bits from the base of the casserole. Add the stock, stirring constantly, and bring to the boil. Bubble for 2–3 minutes. Add the bay leaf and return the meat to the casserole. Cover and cook in the oven for 1½–2 hours until the meat is tender. Check for seasoning and add more salt and pepper if necessary. Remove from the oven and cool. Chill overnight in the refrigerator to develop the flavours. Remove the bay leaf.

3 Preheat the oven to 200°C/400°F/Gas Mark 6.

4 Roll out the pastry on a lightly floured work surface to about 7 cm/2¾ inches larger than the pie dish. Cut off a 3-cm/1¼-inch strip around the edge. Moisten the rim of the dish and press the pastry strip onto it. Place a pie funnel in the centre of the dish and spoon in the meat filling. Don't overfill; keep any extra gravy to serve separately.

5 Moisten the pastry collar with a little water and put on the pastry lid. Crimp the edges of the pastry firmly and glaze with the egg.

6 Bake the pie on a tray near the top of the oven for about 30 minutes. If necessary, cover it with foil and reduce the oven temperature a little. The pie should be golden brown and the filling bubbling hot.

STEAK & KIDNEY PUDDING

Steak and kidney steamed in a suet crust pastry, flavoured with mushrooms and parsley, must be the most British of British meat dishes. Also going by the affectionate cockney name of 'Kate & Sydney', this pudding is traditional all over the British Isles. Initially it was made just with steak, but in the 1860s Mrs Beeton published a recipe using steak and kidney, and it has lasted as such up until now. Sometimes oysters were included in the pudding when they were cheap.

SERVES 4

INGREDIENTS
butter, for greasing
450 g/1 lb braising steak, trimmed and cut into 2.5-cm/ 1-inch pieces
2 lambs' kidneys, cored and cut into 2.5-cm/1-inch pieces
55 g/2 oz flour
1 onion, finely chopped
115 g/4 oz large field mushrooms, sliced (optional)
1 tbsp chopped fresh parsley
300 ml/10 fl oz (approx) stock, or a mixture of beer and water
salt and pepper

SUET PASTRY
350 g/12 oz self-raising flour
175 g/6 oz suet
225 ml/8 fl oz cold water
salt and pepper

1 Grease a 1.2-litre/2-pint pudding basin.

2 Put the prepared meat into a large plastic bag with the flour and salt and pepper and shake well until all the meat is well coated. Add the onion, mushrooms, if using, and the parsley and shake again.

3 Make the suet pastry by mixing the flour, suet and some salt and pepper together. Add enough of the cold water to make a soft dough.

4 Keep a quarter of the dough to one side and roll the remainder out to form a circle big enough to line the pudding basin. Line the basin, making sure that there is a good 1 cm/½ inch hanging over the edge.

5 Place the meat mixture in the basin and pour in enough of the stock to cover the meat.

6 Roll out the remaining pastry to make a lid. Fold in the edges of the pastry, dampen them and place the lid on top. Seal firmly in place.

7 Cover with a piece of greaseproof paper and then foil, with a pleat to allow for expansion during cooking, and seal well. Place in a steamer or large saucepan half-filled with boiling water. Simmer the pudding for 4–5 hours, topping up the water from time to time.

8 Remove the basin from the steamer and take off the coverings. Wrap a clean cloth around the basin and serve at the table.

SHEPHERD'S PIE

Shepherd's pie has always been a nursery and school favourite and is classic, feel-good food. It is simple to prepare and can be made ahead and reheated. Traditionally it was put together from leftover lamb from the Sunday joint and served as a family meal in the week. Using good-quality minced lamb gives a much better flavour. Shepherd's pie is often confused with cottage pie, but that version is always made with minced beef rather than lamb.

SERVES 6

INGREDIENTS
1 tbsp olive oil
2 onions, finely chopped
2 garlic cloves, finely chopped
675 g/1 lb 8 oz good-quality
    minced lamb
2 carrots, finely chopped
1 tbsp plain flour
225 ml/8 fl oz beef or chicken
    stock
125 ml/4 fl oz red wine
Worcestershire sauce (optional)
salt and pepper

MASHED POTATO TOPPING
675 g/1 lb 8 oz floury potatoes,
    such as King Edwards, Maris
    Piper or Desirée, peeled and
    cut into chunks
55 g/2 oz butter
2 tbsp cream or milk
salt and pepper

1 Preheat the oven to 180°C/350°F/Gas Mark 4.

2 Heat the oil in a large flameproof casserole dish and fry the onions until softened, then add the garlic and stir well.

3 Raise the heat and add the meat. Cook quickly to brown the meat all over, stirring continuously. Add the carrots and season well with salt and pepper.

4 Stir in the flour and add the stock and wine. Stir well and heat until simmering and thickened.

5 Cover the casserole dish and cook in the oven for about 1 hour. Check the consistency from time to time and add a little more stock or wine if required. The meat mixture should be quite thick but not dry. Season with salt and pepper to taste and add a little Worcestershire sauce, if using.

6 While the meat is cooking, make the mashed potato topping. Cook the potatoes in a large saucepan of boiling salted water for 15–20 minutes. Drain well and mash with a potato masher until smooth. Add the butter and cream and season well with salt and pepper.

7 Spoon the lamb mixture into an ovenproof serving dish and spread or pipe the potato on top.

8 Increase the oven temperature to 200°C/400°F/Gas Mark 6 and cook the pie for 15–20 minutes at the top of the oven until golden brown. You might like to finish it off under a medium grill for a really crisp brown topping to the potato.

CHICKEN CASSEROLE WITH DUMPLINGS

This one-pot meal, with rich, light, herb-flavoured dumplings, takes the chill off a winter's day and is bursting with flavour. It is also easy to prepare and is ideal for busy cooks with a hungry family to feed. This farmhouse-style recipe uses carrots, leeks, parsnips and turnips, but you can replace one or the other with celeriac or swede, as long as you keep the quantities the same. Although chicken pieces are convenient, this dish will be even more economical if you portion a whole chicken yourself.

SERVES 4

INGREDIENTS
4 chicken quarters
2 tbsp sunflower oil
2 medium leeks
250 g/9 oz carrots, chopped
250 g/9 oz parsnips, chopped
2 small turnips, chopped
600 ml/1 pint chicken stock
3 tbsp Worcestershire sauce
2 sprigs fresh rosemary
salt and pepper

DUMPLINGS
200 g/7 oz self-raising flour
100 g/3½ oz suet
1 tbsp chopped rosemary leaves
cold water, to mix
salt and pepper

1 Remove the skin from the chicken if you prefer. Heat the oil in a large, flameproof casserole or heavy saucepan and fry the chicken until golden. Using a slotted spoon, remove the chicken from the pan. Drain off the excess fat.

2 Trim and slice the leeks. Add the carrots, parsnips and turnips to the casserole and cook for 5 minutes, until lightly coloured. Return the chicken to the pan.

3 Add the chicken stock, Worcestershire sauce, rosemary and seasoning, then bring to the boil.

4 Reduce the heat, cover and simmer gently for about 50 minutes or until the juices run clear when the chicken is pierced with a skewer.

5 To make the dumplings, combine the flour, suet, rosemary and seasoning in a bowl. Stir in just enough cold water to bind to a firm dough.

6 Form into 8 small balls and place on top of the chicken and vegetables. Cover and simmer for a further 10–12 minutes, until the dumplings are well risen. Serve with the casserole.

TOAD IN THE HOLE

I remember toad in the hole as our favourite Saturday lunch, though I never knew where the name came from and, in fact, no one seems to have a reliable answer. Batter puddings are known in many regions and this dish is really just Yorkshire pudding batter cooked around sausages. Although a modest meal, it can be really satisfying, particularly if you take advantage of the wide range of good, well-flavoured sausages available today.

SERVES 4

INGREDIENTS
oil, for greasing
115 g/4 oz plain flour
pinch of salt
1 egg, beaten
300 ml/10 fl oz milk
450 g/1 lb good-quality pork
   sausages
1 tbsp vegetable oil

1 Grease a 20 x 25-cm/8 x 10-inch ovenproof dish or roasting tin.

2 Make the batter by sifting the flour and salt into a mixing bowl. Make a well in the centre and add the beaten egg and half the milk. Carefully stir the liquid into the flour until the mixture is smooth. Gradually beat in the remaining milk. Leave to stand for 30 minutes.

3 Preheat the oven to 220°C/425°F/Gas Mark 7.

4 Prick the sausages and place them in the dish. Sprinkle over the oil and cook the sausages in the oven for 10 minutes until they are beginning to colour and the fat has started to run and is sizzling.

5 Remove from the oven and quickly pour the batter over the sausages. Return to the oven and cook for 35–45 minutes until the batter is well risen and golden brown. Serve immediately.

ACCOMPANIMENT
Toad in the hole is delicious served with Onion Gravy (see page 114) or just a pile of softly fried onions.

SAUSAGES & MASH WITH ONION GRAVY

Sausages with mashed potato must be many people's idea of food heaven. If you buy good-quality sausages, make perfect mash and add a truly rich onion gravy, this is a dish fit for angels. We all have our favourite sausages, be they plain pork, Cumberland or more unusual varieties, like venison. Fry them thoroughly to ensure the insides are cooked and the skin is crisp and sticky, or put them in the oven at 180°C/350°F/Gas Mark 4 for 25–30 minutes.

SERVES 4

INGREDIENTS
8 good-quality sausages
1 tbsp oil

ONION GRAVY
3 onions, cut in half and thinly
   sliced
70 g/2½ oz butter
125 ml/4 fl oz Marsala or port
125 ml/4 fl oz vegetable stock
salt and pepper

MASHED POTATO
900 g/2 lb floury potatoes, such
   as King Edwards, Maris Piper
   or Desirée, peeled and cut into
   chunks
55 g/2 oz butter
3 tbsp hot milk
2 tbsp chopped fresh parsley
salt and pepper

1 Cook the sausages slowly in a frying pan with the oil over a low heat. Cover the pan and turn the sausages from time to time. Don't rush the cooking, because you want them well-cooked and sticky. They will take 25–30 minutes.

2 Meanwhile, prepare the onion gravy by placing the onions in a frying pan with the butter and frying over a low heat until soft, stirring continuously. Continue to cook until they are brown and almost melting, stirring from time to time. This will take about 30 minutes, but it is worth it as the onions will naturally caramelize.

3 Pour in the Marsala and stock and continue to bubble away until the onion gravy is really thick. Season with salt and pepper to taste.

4 To make the mashed potato, cook the potatoes in a large saucepan of boiling salted water for 15–20 minutes. Drain well and mash with a potato masher until smooth. Season with salt and pepper, add the butter, milk and parsley and stir well.

5 Serve the sausages really hot with the mashed potato and the onion gravy spooned over the top.

5 FISH & SEAFOOD

Britain is blessed with some of the world's finest seafood and British cooks have devised many ways to prepare the harvest from the sea. Fish & Chips is a take-away favourite, but there isn't any reason you can't enjoy it at home. For simple, quick cooking, Garlic & Herb Dublin Bay Prawns can't be topped. When you want to impress, try Poached Salmon with Hollandaise Sauce, Roasted Sea Bass and Scallops with Herb Butter.

Smoking fish is also an industry in harbour towns, and Omelette Arnold Bennett showcases tender flakes of smoked haddock. It's ideal for a leisurely breakfast and any leftover smoked fish can be added to home-made Fish Cakes for extra flavour.

FISH & CHIPS

Our great national dish, fish and chips, always seems to feature in childhood memories of food – the time you stayed up to go with an older brother or sister to buy a late supper, or that wet holiday when, drenched to the skin, you bought fish and chips to eat in the rain. I have a friend who always has the ultimate birthday supper: fish and chips on the beach with a bottle of champagne. Try making fish and chips yourself – you will find the home-cooked version totally delicious.

SERVES 2

INGREDIENTS
vegetable oil, for deep-frying
3 large potatoes, such as Cara
    or Desirée
2 thick cod or haddock fillets,
    175 g/6 oz each
175 g/6 oz self-raising flour, plus
    extra for dusting
200 ml/7 fl oz cold lager
salt and pepper
tartare sauce, to serve

1 Heat the oil in a temperature-controlled deep-fat fryer to 120°C/250°F, or in a heavy-based saucepan, checking the temperature with a thermometer, to blanch the chips. Preheat the oven to 150°C/300°F/Gas Mark 2.

2 Peel the potatoes and cut into even-sized chips. Fry for about 8–10 minutes, depending on size, until softened but not coloured. Remove from the oil, drain on kitchen paper and place in a warm dish in the warm oven. Increase the temperature of the oil to 180–190°C/350–375°F, or until a cube of bread browns in 30 seconds.

3 Meanwhile, season the fish with salt and pepper and dust it lightly with a little flour.

4 Make a thick batter by sieving the flour into a bowl with a little salt and whisking in most of the lager. Check the consistency before adding the remainder: it should be very thick like double cream.

5 Dip one fillet into the batter and allow the batter to coat it thickly. Carefully place the fish in the hot oil, then repeat with the other fillet.

6 Cook for 8–10 minutes, depending on the thickness of the fish. Turn the fillets over halfway through the cooking time. Remove the fish from the fryer or saucepan, drain and keep warm.

7 Make sure the oil temperature is still at 180°C/350°F and return the chips to the fryer or saucepan. Cook for a further 2–3 minutes until golden brown and crispy. Drain and season with salt and pepper before serving with the battered fish and tartare sauce.

FISHERMAN'S PIE

Fish pie has been popular everyday comfort food for a long time, and it can be a very fine dish when made with good ingredients and one or two added extras. The addition of some prawns adds to the luxury feel of this pie, as do the mushrooms and fresh herbs. A creamy sauce made with the fish stock and some wine, enriched with cream, makes this a truly special dish. Topped with creamy mashed potato, you have a pie worthy of any dinner party table.

SERVES 6

INGREDIENTS

butter, for greasing
900 g/2 lb white fish fillets, such as plaice, skinned
150 ml/5 fl oz dry white wine
1 tbsp chopped fresh parsley, tarragon or dill
175 g/6 oz small mushrooms, sliced
100 g/3½ oz butter
175 g/6 oz cooked peeled prawns
40 g/1½ oz plain flour
125 ml/4 fl oz double cream
900 g/2 lb floury potatoes, such as King Edwards, Maris Piper or Desirée, peeled and cut into chunks
salt and pepper

1 Preheat the oven to 180°C/350°F/Gas Mark 4. Butter a 1.7-litre/3-pint baking dish.

2 Fold the fish fillets in half and place in the dish. Season well with salt and pepper, pour over the wine and scatter over the herbs.

3 Cover with foil and bake for 15 minutes until the fish starts to flake. Strain off the liquid and reserve for the sauce. Increase the oven temperature to 220°C/425°F/Gas Mark 7.

4 Sauté the mushrooms in a frying pan with 15 g/½ oz of the butter and spoon over the fish. Scatter over the prawns.

5 Heat 55 g/2 oz of the butter in a saucepan and stir in the flour. Cook for a few minutes without browning, remove from the heat, then add the reserved cooking liquid gradually, stirring well between each addition.

6 Return to the heat and gently bring to the boil, still stirring to ensure a smooth sauce. Add the cream and season to taste with salt and pepper. Pour over the fish in the dish and smooth over the surface.

7 Make the mashed potato by cooking the potatoes in boiling salted water for 15–20 minutes. Drain well and mash with a potato masher until smooth. Season to taste with salt and pepper and add the remaining butter, stirring until melted.

8 Pile or pipe the potato onto the fish and sauce and bake for 10–15 minutes until golden brown.

FISH CAKES

Fish cakes used to be a popular children's teatime meal, though ours were always frozen, a bit bland and in need of lots of ketchup. Now they have grown up and become trendy – the texture of fish chunks mixed with well-seasoned creamy potato contrasts well with the crisp coating. You can vary the fish used according to what is available. Smoked haddock is very tasty, while a mixture of smoked and fresh salmon provides a more sophisticated flavour.

SERVES 4

INGREDIENTS

450 g/1 lb floury potatoes, such as King Edwards, Maris Piper or Desirée, peeled and cut into chunks
450 g/1 lb mixed fish fillets, such as cod and salmon, skinned
2 tbsp chopped fresh tarragon
grated rind of 1 lemon
2 tbsp double cream
1 tbsp plain flour
1 egg, beaten
115 g/4 oz breadcrumbs, made from day-old white or wholemeal bread
4 tbsp vegetable oil, for frying
salt and pepper
watercress and lemon wedges, to serve

1 Cook the potatoes in a large saucepan of boiling salted water for 15–20 minutes. Drain well and mash with a potato masher until smooth.

2 Place the fish in a frying pan and just cover with water. Over a medium heat bring to the boil, then reduce the heat, cover and simmer gently for 5 minutes until cooked.

3 Remove from the heat and drain the fish onto a plate. When cool enough to handle, flake the fish roughly into good-sized pieces, ensuring that there are no bones.

4 Mix the potato with the fish, tarragon, lemon rind and cream. Season well with salt and pepper and shape into 4 round cakes or 8 smaller ones.

5 Dust the cakes with flour and dip them into the beaten egg. Coat thoroughly in the breadcrumbs. Place on a baking tray and allow to chill for at least 30 minutes.

6 Heat the oil in the frying pan and fry the cakes over medium heat for 5 minutes on each side, turning them carefully using a palette knife or a fish slice.

7 Serve with the watercress, and lemon wedges for squeezing over the fish cakes.

FLAKY PASTRY FISH PIE

Creamy fish and flaky pastry is a marriage made in heaven. This recipe uses white fish fillets, but you can use other fish if you prefer – a mixture of haddock and smoked haddock is good. The addition of prawns or mussels also works well. England's most famous fish pie came from Cornwall and was called 'Stargazey Pie'. It consisted of small pilchards or herrings, still with their heads on, baked in a pie with the fish heads sticking up through the pastry 'gazing star-wards'!

SERVES 4–6

INGREDIENTS
butter, for greasing
650 g/1 lb 7 oz white fish fillets, such as cod or haddock, skinned
300 ml/10 fl oz milk
1 bay leaf
4 peppercorns
1 small onion, finely sliced
40 g/1½ oz butter
40 g/1½ oz plain flour, plus extra for dusting
1 tbsp chopped fresh parsley or tarragon
150 ml/5 fl oz single cream
2 hard-boiled eggs, roughly chopped
400 g/14 oz ready-made puff pastry
1 egg, beaten
salt and pepper

1 Preheat the oven to 200°C/400°F/Gas Mark 6. Butter a 1.2-litre/2-pint pie dish.

2 Place the fish in a frying pan and cover with the milk. Add the bay leaf, peppercorns and onion slices. Bring to the boil, reduce the heat and simmer gently for 10–12 minutes.

3 Remove from the heat and strain off the milk into a measuring jug. Add a little extra milk if necessary to make the liquid up to 300 ml/10 fl oz. Take out the fish and flake into large pieces, removing any bones.

4 Melt the butter in a saucepan and add the flour. Stir well and cook over a low heat for 2–3 minutes. Remove from the heat and gradually stir in the reserved milk, beating well after each addition. Return the pan to the heat and cook, stirring continuously, until thickened. Continue to cook for 2–3 minutes until smooth and glossy. Season to taste, and add the parsley and cream.

5 Place the fish in the bottom of the pie dish, then add the eggs and season with salt and pepper. Pour the sauce over the fish and mix carefully.

6 Roll out the pastry on a lightly floured surface until just larger than the pie dish. Cut off a strip 1 cm/½ inch wide from around the edge. Moisten the rim of the dish with water and press the pastry strip onto it. Moisten the pastry collar and put on the pastry lid. Crimp the edges firmly and glaze with the egg. If desired, garnish with the leftover pastry shaped into leaves.

7 Place the pie on a baking tray and bake near the top of the oven for 20–25 minutes. Cover with foil if getting too brown.

POACHED SALMON WITH HOLLANDAISE SAUCE

Salmon has always been known as the king of fish and is very versatile. A whole salmon makes a stunning centrepiece for a buffet or a family celebration and is a classic summer party dish that makes a perfect partner for sparkling wine. This recipe poaches the whole salmon in the oven rather than in a fish kettle on the hob, and is suitable for fish under 2.25 kg/5 lb in weight. However, if you do own a fish kettle, the traditional method works just as well.

SERVES 8

INGREDIENTS
melted butter, for greasing
1.8 kg/4 lb whole fresh salmon, gutted
1 lemon, sliced
sprigs of fresh parsley
125 ml/4 fl oz white wine or water
salt and pepper

HOLLANDAISE SAUCE
2 tbsp white wine vinegar
2 tbsp water
6 black peppercorns
3 egg yolks
250 g/9 oz unsalted butter
2 tsp lemon juice
salt and pepper

1 Preheat the oven to 150°C/300°F/Gas Mark 2. Line a large roasting tin with a double layer of foil and brush with butter.

2 Trim off the fins then season the salmon with salt and pepper, inside and out. Lay on the foil and place the lemon slices and parsley in the body cavity. Pour over the wine and gather up the foil to make a fairly loose parcel.

3 Bake for 50–60 minutes. Test the salmon with the point of a knife: the flesh should flake when the fish is cooked. Remove from the oven and leave to stand for 15 minutes before removing from the foil to serve hot. To serve cold, leave for 1–2 hours until lukewarm then carefully remove from the foil and peel away the skin from the top side, leaving the head and tail intact.

4 Meanwhile, to make the hollandaise sauce, put the wine vinegar and water into a small saucepan with the peppercorns, bring to the boil, then reduce the heat and simmer until it is reduced to 1 tablespoon (take care: this happens very quickly). Strain.

5 Mix the egg yolks in a blender or food processor and add the strained vinegar while the machine is running.

6 Melt the butter in a small saucepan and heat until it almost turns brown. Again, while the blender is running, add three quarters of the butter, the lemon juice, then the remaining butter and season well with salt and pepper.

7 Turn the sauce into a serving bowl or keep warm for up to 1 hour in a bowl over a pan of warm water. To serve cold, allow to cool and store in the refrigerator for up to 2 days. Serve the sauce on the side with the salmon.

ROASTED SEA BASS

Roasting is my favourite way to cook a whole fish – it not only looks good, but also picks up other flavours beautifully. You can use either small individual fish to serve as single portions or one large one to share among family or friends. Round fish like sea bass, sea bream, red mullet, red snapper, trout and mackerel are particularly good for roasting as their skin crisps up well while the flesh stays deliciously moist and creamy. Make sure you use really fresh fish if you want this dish to sparkle.

SERVES 4

INGREDIENTS

1.3–1.8 kg/3–4 lb whole sea bass, gutted
1 small onion, finely chopped
2 garlic cloves, finely chopped
2 tbsp finely chopped fresh herbs, such as parsley, chervil and tarragon
25 g/1 oz anchovy fillets, finely chopped
25 g/1 oz butter
150 ml/5 fl oz white wine
2 tbsp crème fraîche
salt and pepper

1 Preheat the oven to 200°C/400°F/Gas Mark 6.

2 Remove any scales from the fish and clean it thoroughly both inside and out. If desired, trim off the fins with a pair of scissors. Using a sharp knife, make five or six cuts diagonally into the flesh of the fish on both sides. Season well with salt and pepper, both inside and out.

3 Mix the onion, garlic, herbs and anchovies together in a bowl.

4 Stuff the fish with half the mixture and spoon the remainder into a roasting tin. Place the sea bass on top.

5 Spread the butter over the sea bass, pour over the wine and place in the oven. Roast for 30–35 minutes until the fish is cooked through.

6 Remove the fish from the tin to a warmed serving dish. Return the tin to the top of the stove and stir the onion mixture and juices together over a medium heat. Add the crème fraîche and pour into a warmed serving bowl.

7 Serve the sea bass whole and divide at the table. Spoon a little sauce on the side.

VARIATIONS
Red mullet, weighing 280–350 g/10–12 oz each, will take only 15–20 minutes to roast. Serve 1 per person. Brush well with butter and stuff simply with some herbs and lemon slices.

SCALLOPS WITH HERB BUTTER

Scallops are the most delicate of shellfish, creamy in texture and with a sweet flavour. They hardly need any cooking and although expensive you don't need many: 3–4 per person are sufficient. In the past, scallops tended to be served with rich sauces, but today simplicity is the key and a quick sear in a hot frying pan or on a griddle is all they need. Most scallops come with their orange coral. You can cook these at the same time or keep them (frozen) to flavour fish pies or sauces.

SERVES 3–4

INGREDIENTS
12 large shelled scallops, cleaned
1 tbsp vegetable oil
salt and pepper
crusty bread, to serve

HERB BUTTER
25 g/1 oz unsalted butter
2 garlic cloves, finely chopped
2 tbsp chopped fresh parsley

VARIATION
Scallops with Crushed Beans & Rocket Salad
Fry 1 finely chopped garlic clove in 1 tablespoon olive oil in a small saucepan. Add a pinch of dried crushed chillies and mix well. Drain 400 g/14 oz canned flageolet beans and add to the pan with 125 ml/4 fl oz white wine. Bring to the boil and crush the beans with a wooden spoon until you have a rough paste, adding a little water to make a loose purée, and season with salt and pepper to taste. Divide the purée among 4 warm serving dishes and place the cooked scallops on top. Serve with a rocket salad dressed simply with olive oil and lemon juice.

1 Cut away any discoloured parts from the scallops. Dry well and season with salt and pepper.

2 Heat a heavy-based frying pan or griddle and brush with the oil. When the oil is smoking, add the scallops and cook for 1 minute, then turn and cook on the other side for 1 minute. It is a good idea to cook the scallops in 2 batches, as if you try to cook them all at once you might end up with them stewing rather than frying. The scallops should have a good golden colour and a slight crust at the edges. Transfer to a warm plate and keep warm.

3 To make the herb butter, melt the butter in a saucepan and fry the garlic for a few seconds. Add the parsley and, while still foaming, pour over the scallops.

4 Serve at once with plenty of crusty bread to mop up the juices.

GARLIC & HERB DUBLIN BAY PRAWNS

Dublin Bay prawns are also known as langoustines or scampi. Breaded and fried scampi are great favourites with the British, but fresh Dublin Bay prawns are now also more readily available from Scotland and abroad. You can, however, use jumbo prawns if you can't find langoustines. Dublin Bay prawns are simply delicious served grilled or fried in herb butter, with a glass of cold Sauvignon. In seaside pubs they are sometimes served cold in a pint glass and washed down with beer.

SERVES 2

INGREDIENTS

12 raw Dublin Bay prawns in their shells
juice of ½ lemon
2 garlic cloves, crushed
3 tbsp chopped fresh parsley
1 tbsp chopped fresh dill
3 tbsp softened butter
salt and pepper
lemon wedges and crusty bread, to serve

1 Rinse and peel the prawns. Devein, using a sharp knife to slice along the back from the head end to the tail, and removing the thin black intestine.

2 Mix the lemon juice with the garlic, herbs and butter to form a paste. Season well with the salt and pepper. Spread the paste over the prawns and leave to marinate for 30 minutes.

3 Cook the prawns under a preheated medium grill for 5–6 minutes. Alternatively, heat a frying pan and fry the prawns in the paste until cooked. Turn out onto hot plates and pour over the pan juices. Serve at once with lemon wedges and some crusty bread.

VARIATIONS
To make a more substantial meal, serve the prawns with some fine spaghetti or angel hair pasta. Dublin Bay prawns can also be served cold in a salad. Try mixing 125 g/4½ oz cooked Dublin Bay prawns with 280 g/10 oz cubed melon and a cubed avocado. Dress with 4 tablespoons lime juice and 1 tablespoon Thai fish sauce and add a pinch of sugar. Mix well and garnish with chopped fresh coriander.

GOUJONS OF SOLE

'Goujons' comes from the French *goujon*, which means a small freshwater fish. In the British usage, however, whenever you see the word it means small, deep-fried pieces of fish fillet. Flatfish, such as sole or plaice, are ideal, but you can use other white fish, cut into equal, finger-sized pieces. Ideally, these golden pieces of fish should be served as soon as they are fried, but they can be kept warm in a low oven for 20 minutes or so. If you leave them too long, however, they will become soggy.

SERVES 2

INGREDIENTS
6 tbsp mayonnaise
2 garlic cloves, crushed
2 large sole fillets, skinned
1 egg, beaten
3 tbsp plain flour
vegetable oil, for deep-frying
lemon wedges, to garnish

1 Combine the mayonnaise and garlic in a small dish. Cover with clingfilm and refrigerate while you cook the fish.

2 Cut the fish into 2.5-cm/1-inch strips. Dip the strips in the egg, then drain and dredge in flour.

3 Meanwhile, heat the oil in a deep-fryer or large saucepan to 180–190°C/350–375°F, or until a cube of bread browns in 30 seconds. Fry the pieces of fish in the hot oil for 3–4 minutes, or until golden brown. Remove from the oil and drain on a dish lined with kitchen paper.

4 Remove the garlic mayonnaise from the refrigerator and stir once. Pile the goujons into a warm dish, garnish with lemon wedges and serve with the mayonnaise on the side for dipping.

GRILLED MUSHROOM & SPINACH-STUFFED TROUT

Grilling or barbecuing fish is one of the best ways to preserve all its flavour, particularly when it has been freshly landed at a British fishing port. Whole freshwater fish, preferably caught yourself, is also very good cooked simply on a grill or even on the spot over an open wood fire – the added aroma of the woodsmoke is a delicious bonus. To enhance the taste, the fish should be gutted and cleaned and a mixture of subtle herbs and flavourings stuffed into the body cavity.

SERVES 2

INGREDIENTS
2 whole trout, about 350 g/
    12 oz each, gutted
1 tbsp vegetable oil
salt and pepper

STUFFING
25 g/1 oz butter
2 shallots, finely chopped
55 g/2 oz mushrooms, finely
    chopped
55 g/2 oz baby spinach
1 tbsp chopped fresh parsley or
    tarragon
grated rind of 1 lemon
whole nutmeg, for grating

TOMATO SALSA
2 tomatoes, peeled, deseeded
    and finely diced
10-cm/4-inch piece cucumber,
    finely diced
2 spring onions, finely chopped
1 tbsp olive oil
salt and pepper

1 Clean the trout, trim the fins with a pair of scissors and wipe the inside of the fish with kitchen paper. Leave the head and tail on and slash the skin of each fish on both sides about 5 times. Brush with the oil and season well with salt and pepper, both inside and out.

2 To make the stuffing, melt the butter in a small saucepan and gently soften the shallots for 2–3 minutes. Add the mushrooms and continue to cook for a further 2 minutes. Add the spinach and heat until it is just wilted.

3 Remove from the heat and add the parsley, lemon rind and a good grating of nutmeg. Allow to cool.

4 Fill the trout with the mushroom and spinach stuffing, then reshape them as neatly as you can.

5 Grill under a medium grill for 10–12 minutes, turning once. The skin should be brown and crispy. Alternatively, barbecue for 6–8 minutes on each side, depending on the heat.

6 To make the tomato salsa, mix together all the ingredients and season well with salt and pepper.

7 Serve the trout hot with the tomato salsa spooned over them.

OMELETTE ARNOLD BENNETT

We tend to associate omelettes with France, but they have, in fact, been known since the sixteenth century in Britain. This omelette, named after the novelist Arnold Bennett, is rather an extravagant affair. The original version was devised in the 1930s by the chef of the Savoy Hotel in London for the author, who regularly dined there. It is said that Bennett liked it so much that he ordered it every time he visited the hotel. Some recipes add a hollandaise sauce, but I prefer it without.

SERVES 2

INGREDIENTS
175 g/6 oz undyed smoked
   haddock, skinned
25 g/1 oz butter
4 eggs
1 tbsp olive oil
4 tbsp single cream
2 tbsp grated Cheddar
   or Parmesan cheese
salt and pepper

1 Place the fish in a large saucepan and cover with water. Bring the water to the boil, then turn down to a simmer and poach the fish for 8–10 minutes until it flakes easily. Remove from the heat and drain onto a plate. When cool enough to handle, flake the fish and remove any bones.

2 Melt half the butter in a small saucepan and add the haddock, to warm.

3 Beat the eggs together gently with a fork and season carefully with salt and pepper, taking care not to add too much salt because the haddock will already be quite salty.

4 Melt the remaining butter with the oil in a 23-cm/9-inch frying pan over a medium heat. When the butter starts to froth, pour in the eggs and spread them around by tilting the frying pan. Use a spatula or fork to move the egg around until it is cooked underneath but still liquid on top.

5 Tip in the hot haddock and spread over the omelette.

6 Pour over the cream and top with the cheese, then place the frying pan under a hot grill for 1 minute until the cheese is melted. Serve immediately on hot plates.

VARIATIONS
You can make individual omelettes using a smaller pan and 2–3 eggs per person. A more elaborate omelette can also be made with the addition of hollandaise sauce.

6 VEGETABLES & SIDES

Seasonal vegetables have always played a major role in traditional British meals. Once this might have been to bulk out the more expensive meat, but now it is more likely to be out of appreciation of how vital vegetables are to a healthy diet. Potatoes and other root vegetables are always popular, and you'll find plenty of essential recipes in this chapter, from how to make the Perfect Roast Potatoes and Perfect Mash to Roasted Root Vegetables and Neeps & Tatties. Colcannon and Bubble & Squeak are traditional ways to transform leftovers into satisfying meals. You'll also find plenty of ways to add excitement to the salad bowl.

PERFECT ROAST POTATOES

Perfect roast potatoes are crisp on the outside and soft and fluffy on the inside. Do choose the right potatoes – floury ones are best. The choice of fat is also important – goose or duck fat gives an amazing flavour. However, the fat from a joint is almost as good and really tasty potatoes can also be made using olive oil. Parboiling the potatoes is a chore but worthwhile because it gives crispy outsides. A heavy roasting tin and a hot oven are also essential for success.

SERVES 6

INGREDIENTS

1.3 kg/3 lb large floury potatoes, such as King Edwards, Maris Piper or Desirée, peeled and cut into even-sized chunks
3 tbsp dripping, goose fat, duck fat or olive oil
salt

1 Preheat the oven to 220°C/425°F/Gas Mark 7.

2 Cook the potatoes in a large saucepan of boiling salted water over a medium heat, covered, for 5–7 minutes. They will still be firm. Remove from the heat.

3 Meanwhile, add the fat to a roasting tin and place in the hot oven.

4 Drain the potatoes well and return them to the saucepan. Cover with the lid and firmly shake the pan so that the surface of the potatoes is roughened to help give a much crisper texture.

5 Remove the roasting tin from the oven and carefully tip the potatoes into the hot oil. Baste them to ensure they are all coated with the oil.

6 Roast at the top of the oven for 45–50 minutes until they are browned all over and thoroughly crisp. Turn the potatoes and baste again only once during the process or the crunchy edges will be destroyed.

7 Carefully transfer the potatoes from the roasting tin into a hot serving dish. Sprinkle with a little salt and serve at once. Any leftovers (although this is most unlikely) are delicious cold.

VARIATION

Small whole unpeeled new potatoes are delicious roasted too. They don't need any parboiling – just coat them with the hot fat and then roast for 30–40 minutes. Drain well and season with salt and pepper before serving.

PERFECT MASH

Mashed potato is Britain's longest-standing comfort food – almost everyone loves smooth, creamy mashed potato. But it has to be smooth and creamy, not lumpy. Using the right potato is essential – you need floury potatoes, such as King Edwards, or a good all-rounder, like the Desirée. A potato masher is invaluable but I prefer a potato ricer, which presses the potato through tiny holes and makes fine 'worms' which means you never get lumps.

SERVES 4

INGREDIENTS
900 g/2 lb floury potatoes, such as King Edwards, Maris Piper or Desirée
55 g/2 oz butter
3 tbsp hot milk
salt and pepper

1 Peel the potatoes, placing them in cold water as you prepare the others to prevent them from going brown.

2 Cut the potatoes into even-sized chunks and cook in a large saucepan of boiling salted water over a medium heat, covered, for 20–25 minutes until they are tender. Test with the point of a knife, but do make sure you test right to the middle to avoid lumps.

3 Remove the pan from the heat and drain the potatoes. Return the potatoes to the hot pan and mash with a potato masher until smooth.

4 Add the butter and continue to mash until it is all mixed in, then add the milk (it is better hot because the potatoes absorb it more quickly to produce a creamier mash).

5 Taste the mash and season with salt and pepper as necessary. Serve at once.

VARIATIONS
For herb mash, mix in 3 tablespoons chopped fresh parsley, thyme or mint. For mustard or horseradish mash, mix in 2 tablespoons wholegrain mustard or horseradish sauce. For pesto mash, stir in 4 tablespoons fresh pesto and for nutmeg mash, grate ½ a nutmeg into the mash and add 125 ml/4 fl oz natural yogurt. To make creamed potato, add 125 ml/4 fl oz soured cream and 2 tablespoons snipped fresh chives.

NEEPS & TATTIES

This tasty dish, from Scotland, is traditionally served with haggis on Burns Night.There is always a great debate amongst cooks as to whether 'neeps' are turnips or swedes. Turnips are white root vegetables and swedes are the larger orange-coloured ones. Most recipes are interchangeable, but for this one I find the coloured swedes are better. 'Bashed neeps' are mashed swedes and are mixed with mashed potato to make the neeps and tatties.

SERVES 4–5

INGREDIENTS

450 g/1 lb swedes, peeled and
    diced
250 g/9 oz floury potatoes, such
    as King Edwards, Maris Piper or
    Desirée, peeled and diced
55 g/2 oz butter
whole nutmeg, for grating
salt and pepper
fresh parsley sprigs, to garnish

1 Cook the swede and potato in a large saucepan of boiling salted water for 20 minutes until soft. Test with the point of a knife and if not cooked return to the heat for a further 5 minutes.

2 Drain well, return to the rinsed-out pan and heat for a few moments to ensure they are dry. Mash using a potato masher until smooth. Season well with salt and pepper and add the butter. Grate as much of the nutmeg into the mash as you like and serve piping hot, garnished with the parsley.

COLCANNON

Potatoes have always been the staple food of Ireland and have been made into many great dishes. Cabbage and kale are also common ingredients and are mixed together in many recipes. Colcannon is a traditional Irish dish often served at Halloween, when lucky charms would be hidden in the mixture (rather like in a Christmas pudding) and those who found them might expect a proposal of marriage. Leeks or spring onions are often added as a variation.

SERVES 3–4

INGREDIENTS
225 g/8 oz green or white
   cabbage
6 spring onions, cut into
   5-mm/¼-inch pieces
salt and pepper
55 g/2 oz butter, cut into
   3–4 pieces, to serve

MASHED POTATO
450 g/1 lb floury potatoes,
   such as King Edwards, Maris
   Piper or Desirée, peeled and
   cut into chunks
55 g/2 oz butter
150 ml/5 fl oz single cream
salt and pepper

1 To make the mashed potato, cook the potatoes in a large saucepan of boiling salted water for 15–20 minutes. Drain well and mash with a potato masher until smooth. Season with salt and pepper, add the butter and cream and stir well. The potato should be very soft.

2 Cut the cabbage into quarters, remove the centre stalk and shred finely.

3 Cook the cabbage in a large saucepan of boiling salted water for just 1–2 minutes until it is soft. Drain thoroughly.

4 Mix the potato and cabbage together and stir in the spring onion. Season well with salt and pepper.

5 Serve in individual bowls and top with a good piece of butter.

VARIATIONS
This is a totally vegetarian dish and can be eaten on its own or with some grated cheese added. It is also delicious served with cold sliced meats or hot sausages and crisply fried lardons of bacon can be added to give more flavour.

ASPARAGUS WITH MELTED BUTTER

Fresh asparagus is considered a delicacy owing to its relatively short season: May to early July. It has been grown in Britain for centuries, particularly in the Vale of Evesham. It is labour-intensive to produce and its growing habit means that the plants are only productive for half their lives. We eat green asparagus, but in France and Belgium the white variety is more valued. Asparagus can be steamed, boiled, grilled or roasted, and served simply with butter or hollandaise sauce.

SERVES 2

INGREDIENTS
16–20 stalks of asparagus,
  trimmed to about 20 cm/
  8 inches
85 g/3 oz unsalted butter, melted
sea salt and pepper, to serve

1 Remove some of the base of the asparagus stalks with a potato peeler if they are rather thick.

2 Tie the stalks together with string or use a wire basket so that they can easily be removed from the pan without damage.

3 Bring a large saucepan of salted water to the boil and plunge in the stalks. Cover with a lid and cook for 4–5 minutes. Pierce one stalk near the base with a sharp knife. If it is fairly soft remove from the heat at once. Do not overcook asparagus or the tender tips will fall off.

4 Drain the asparagus thoroughly and serve on large warm plates with the butter poured over or in a separate bowl for dipping. Both the butter and the asparagus should be warm rather than hot. Serve with salt and pepper and hand out large napkins!

VARIATIONS
To griddle asparagus, brush a griddle with oil and then heat until it is very hot. Place the asparagus on the griddle and cook for 2 minutes on one side, then turn over and griddle for a further 2 minutes. Serve immediately. Asparagus is also delicious served with hollandaise sauce, slices of Parma ham, shavings of Parmesan cheese or soft-boiled quail eggs. Alternatively, fry 55 g/2 oz fresh white breadcrumbs in 40 g/1½ oz butter until golden and crisp and serve scattered over lightly cooked asparagus.

ROASTED ONIONS

Onions form an important part of savoury cooking. Chopped or sliced and fried, they are the base of all casserole dishes and many soup recipes. But cooked on their own, they can be a meal in themselves and are very healthy. Onions are easy to grow and are now found all over the British Isles, but I still remember the 'onion men' from Brittany who used to travel across to Britain with their strings of onions on their bicycles. Sadly this selling practice has all but ceased.

SERVES 4

INGREDIENTS
8 large onions, peeled
3 tbsp olive oil
55 g/2 oz butter
2 tsp chopped fresh thyme
200 g/7 oz Cheddar or
  Lancashire cheese, grated
salt and pepper
salad and crusty bread, to serve

1 Preheat the oven to 180°C/350°F/ Gas Mark 4.

2 Cut a cross down through the top of the onions towards the root, without cutting all the way through.

3 Place the onions in a roasting tin and drizzle over the olive oil.

4 Press a little of the butter into the open crosses, sprinkle with the thyme and season with salt and pepper. Cover with foil and roast for 40–45 minutes.

5 Remove from the oven, take off the foil and baste the onions with the pan juices. Return to the oven and cook for a further 15 minutes, uncovered, to allow the onions to brown.

6 Take the onions out of the oven and scatter the grated cheese over them. Return them to the oven for a few minutes so that the cheese starts to melt.

7 Serve at once with some salad and lots of warm crusty bread.

VARIATIONS
Stuffed Onions
Preheat the oven to 220°C/425°F/ Gas Mark 7. Peel 4 onions and boil in salted water for 20 minutes. Scoop out the centres of the onions and stuff with a mixture of 55 g/2 oz each grated cheese and breadcrumbs and 1 teaspoon mustard. Place the stuffed onions in a baking dish, top with 25 g/ 1 oz butter and bake in the oven for 25–30 minutes. Serve hot as a starter or as an accompaniment to roast meat.

ROASTED ROOT VEGETABLES

Root vegetables are our winter staples. They keep well and can be cooked in various ways. Roasted root vegetables are particularly popular since they all cook together and need little attention once prepared. You can use whatever is available: potatoes, parsnips, turnips, swedes, carrots and, though not strictly root vegetables, squash and onions. I like to use a good handful of herbs, particularly the stronger flavoured ones like rosemary, thyme and sage.

SERVES 4–6

INGREDIENTS

3 parsnips, peeled and cut into 5-cm/2-inch pieces
4 baby turnips, quartered
3 carrots, peeled and cut into 5-cm/2-inch pieces
450 g/1 lb butternut squash, peeled and cut into 5-cm/2-inch chunks
450 g/1 lb sweet potato, peeled and cut into 5-cm/2-inch chunks
2 garlic cloves, finely chopped
2 tbsp chopped fresh rosemary
2 tbsp chopped fresh thyme
2 tsp chopped fresh sage
3 tbsp olive oil
salt and pepper
2 tbsp chopped fresh mixed herbs, such as parsley, thyme and mint, to garnish

1 Preheat the oven to 220°C/425°F/Gas Mark 7.

2 Arrange all the vegetables in a single layer in a large roasting tin. Scatter over the garlic and the herbs.

3 Pour over the oil and season well with salt and pepper.

4 Toss all the ingredients together until they are well mixed and coated with the oil (you can leave them to marinate at this stage to allow the flavours to be absorbed).

5 Roast at the top of the oven for 50–60 minutes until the vegetables are cooked and nicely browned. Turn the vegetables over halfway through the cooking time.

6 Serve with a good handful of fresh herbs scattered on top and a final sprinkling of salt and pepper.

VARIATIONS

Shallots or wedges of red onion can be added to the root vegetables to give additional flavour and texture. Whole cloves of unpeeled garlic are also good roasted with the other vegetables. You can then squeeze out the creamy cooked garlic over the vegetables before eating them.

SWEET & SOUR RED CABBAGE

Cabbage was known in the time of the ancient Egyptians, but only in the last century have we had so many varieties available in Britain. Most people can remember when it was served overcooked at school, but luckily we now cook cabbage for shorter times and without so much water. Red cabbage can be eaten raw and made into coleslaw, but it is best when cooked with apples and wine vinegar and flavoured with spices and redcurrant jelly.

SERVES 6–8

INGREDIENTS

1 red cabbage, about 750 g/
    1 lb 10 oz
2 tbsp olive oil
2 onions, finely sliced
1 garlic clove, chopped
2 small cooking apples, peeled,
    cored and sliced
2 tbsp muscovado sugar
½ tsp ground cinnamon
1 tsp crushed juniper berries
whole nutmeg, for grating
2 tbsp red wine vinegar
grated rind and juice of 1 orange
2 tbsp redcurrant jelly
salt and pepper

1 Cut the cabbage into quarters, remove the centre stalk and shred the leaves finely.

2 Pour the oil into a large saucepan and add the red cabbage, onions, garlic and apples.

3 Sprinkle on the sugar, cinnamon and juniper berries and grate a quarter of the nutmeg into the pan.

4 Pour over the red wine vinegar and orange juice and add the orange rind.

5 Stir well and season with salt and pepper. The saucepan will be quite full but the volume of the cabbage will reduce during cooking.

6 Cook over medium heat, stirring well from time to time, until the cabbage is just tender but still has 'bite'. This will take 10–15 minutes depending on how finely the cabbage is sliced.

7 Stir in the redcurrant jelly and add more salt and pepper if necessary. Serve hot.

COOK'S TIP
Red cabbage is a traditional accompaniment for game and meat dishes. It is also truly delicious served with sausages for a simple supper.

CAULIFLOWER CHEESE

Cauliflower cheese is nutritious, suitable for vegetarians and quite inexpensive. For a more substantial dish, add fried onions and bacon before the cheese sauce. A mixture of broccoli and cauliflower can be used to give a variation of flavours and textures. Sometimes wholemeal breadcrumbs are added to the Parmesan cheese to give a crunchier topping. This dish is sometimes described as cauliflower 'au gratin' – a French term for a dish topped with cheese and browned under a grill.

SERVES 4

INGREDIENTS
1 cauliflower, trimmed and cut into florets (675 g/1 lb 8 oz prepared weight)
40 g/1½ oz butter
40 g/1½ oz plain flour
450 ml/16 fl oz milk
115 g/4 oz Cheddar cheese, finely grated
whole nutmeg, for grating
1 tbsp grated Parmesan cheese
salt and pepper

1 Cook the cauliflower in a saucepan of boiling salted water for 4–5 minutes. It should still be firm. Drain, place in a hot 1.4-litre/2½-pint gratin dish and keep warm.

2 Melt the butter in the rinsed-out saucepan over a medium heat and stir in the flour. Cook for 1 minute, stirring continuously.

3 Remove from the heat and stir in the milk gradually until you have a smooth consistency.

4 Return to a low heat and continue to stir while the sauce comes to the boil and thickens. Reduce the heat and simmer gently, stirring constantly, for about 3 minutes until the sauce is creamy and smooth.

5 Remove from the heat and stir in the Cheddar cheese and a good grating of the nutmeg. Taste and season well with salt and pepper.

6 Pour the hot sauce over the cauliflower, top with the Parmesan and place under a hot grill to brown. Serve immediately.

PEASE PUDDING

'Pease pudding hot, pease pudding cold, pease pudding in the pot, nine days old' refers to a pudding of dried split peas. The British have always preferred peas over other pulses and this dish was popular with poor and rich alike. Originally an accompaniment to boiled ham or bacon, the pudding was boiled in a cloth with the ham. Today it is easily made with a few extra flavourings and steamed in a pudding basin. Eat it freshly made, or serve sliced and fried on subsequent days.

SERVES 4–6

INGREDIENTS
350 g/12 oz dried split green
    peas
1 carrot, finely diced (optional)
1 celery stick, finely diced
    (optional)
1 onion, finely chopped (optional)
2 tsp vegetable stock powder
55 g/2 oz butter
1 tbsp chopped fresh mixed
    herbs
1 egg, beaten
salt and pepper
boiled ham or gammon, to serve

1 Wash the peas well. Some dried varieties require soaking – follow directions provided on the pack.

2 Drain the peas, place in a saucepan and cover with fresh water. Place the saucepan over a medium heat and bring to the boil. Add the vegetables, if using, and the stock powder. If you have any meat bones, you could add these. Cook gently for 30–45 minutes until the peas are tender.

3 Remove from the heat and drain off the liquid (this can be retained to make soup). Remove and discard any bones.

4 Purée the pea mixture using a mouli sieve or a food processor. Season well with salt and pepper and beat in the butter, herbs and the egg.

5 Spoon the mixture into a greased 600 ml/1 pint pudding basin, cover with greaseproof paper and foil and steam for 1 hour. Turn out the pudding and serve with boiled ham or gammon.

VARIATIONS
Mushy Peas
Put 450 g/1 lb whole dried peas into a saucepan with 1 finely chopped onion, 1 finely chopped carrot and a small bunch of mixed fresh herbs. Cover with water, bring to the boil very slowly and simmer very gently for 2 hours. Strain the peas, discard the herbs and mash the peas and vegetables with a potato masher. Add 55 g/2 oz butter, beat into the mixture and season well with salt and pepper. Serve hot with duck, pork or fish and chips.

BUBBLE & SQUEAK

This is the English way of using up leftover potatoes and vegetables, with similar recipes coming from Ireland and Scotland. These filling dishes come from a time when careful housewives made sure they used up all their leftovers. This recipe can also be made from fresh potatoes and cabbage and is all the more delicious for it. You can use sliced potatoes, but I prefer using mashed potato. The name comes from the bubbling sound of the potato in the fat and the squeak of the cabbage.

SERVES 2–3

INGREDIENTS
450 g/1 lb green cabbage
1 onion, thinly sliced
4 tbsp olive oil
salt and pepper

MASHED POTATO
450 g/1 lb floury potatoes, such as King Edwards, Maris Piper or Desirée, peeled and cut into chunks
55 g/2 oz butter
3 tbsp hot milk
salt and pepper

1 To make the mashed potato, cook the potatoes in a large saucepan of boiling salted water for 15–20 minutes. Drain well and mash with a potato masher until smooth. Season with salt and pepper, add the butter and milk and stir well.

2 Cut the cabbage into quarters, remove the centre stalk and shred the leaves finely.

3 In a large frying pan, fry the onion in half the oil until soft. Add the cabbage to the pan and stir-fry for 2–3 minutes until softened. Season with salt and pepper, add the mashed potato and mix together well.

4 Press the mixture firmly into the frying pan and allow to cook over a high heat for 4–5 minutes so that the base is crispy. Place a plate over the frying pan and invert the pan so that the potato cake falls onto the plate. Add the remaining oil to the pan, reheat and slip the cake back into the pan with the uncooked side down.

5 Continue to cook for a further 5 minutes until the bottom is crispy too. Turn out onto a hot plate and cut into wedges for serving. Serve at once.

VARIATIONS
This dish can be made with curly kale or Brussels sprouts instead of the cabbage. The potato and cabbage mix can also be formed into small cakes and fried separately like fish cakes. This is a good way for children to be encouraged to eat cabbage. Bubble & Squeak can also be served with bacon and eggs for breakfast.

FINDING mushrooms growing wild is a real joy. If you've got a good eye and you know which varieties are edible, you can go out for a walk in the morning and come home with your breakfast, lunch or dinner. Sadly, these days it is not often you come across enough mushrooms to take home to cook. Luckily we can now find many varieties of mushrooms in the supermarkets that are cultivated, available throughout the year and can be used in a variety of dishes.

WAYS WITH MUSHROOMS

MUSHROOMS IN RED WINE

Heat 25 g/1 oz butter in a frying pan, add 4 finely chopped shallots and 2 finely chopped garlic cloves. Cook for 1–2 minutes until the shallots are soft. Add 100 g/ 3½ oz whole shiitake mushrooms and the same weight of whole small chestnut mushrooms to the pan and stir well. Pour in 175 ml/6 fl oz beef or vegetable stock and 175 ml/6 fl oz red wine with 1 tablespoon chopped fresh thyme and allow to simmer until the sauce has reduced by half and the mushrooms are soft. Serve immediately. This can be served as a starter or as an accompaniment to steak. Serves 3–4.

BAKED MUSHROOMS

Preheat the oven to 200°C/400°F/ Gas Mark 6. Wipe 4 large flat mushrooms and cut out their stalks. Place the mushrooms in a baking dish and sprinkle over 2 finely chopped garlic cloves and 1 tablespoon finely chopped fresh thyme. Spoon in 4 tablespoons melted butter and squeeze in the juice of 1 lemon. Drizzle over 2 tablespoons olive oil and bake in the oven for 20–25 minutes, basting from time to time. These can be served with couscous or rice to make a good vegetarian supper dish, or with grilled meats or simply on toast. Serves 2.

MUSHROOM RISOTTO

Fry 55 g/2 oz chopped streaky bacon in a large frying pan with 1 finely chopped onion, 25 g/1 oz butter and 1 tablespoon olive oil until the onion is a pale golden colour and the bacon has started to brown. Add 350 g/12 oz risotto rice and stir well. Have ready 1 litre/1¾ pints hot vegetable stock and slowly add a ladleful to the rice. Allow the rice to absorb the stock before adding the next ladleful, stirring constantly. Continue slowly adding stock until it is all used up: this will take 15–20 minutes. Stir in 175 g/6 oz sliced mushrooms. (It is nice to use more exotic ones in this recipe if you can find them, like ceps, morels or shiitake. Otherwise use chestnut or field mushrooms). Allow to cook until the mushrooms have reduced and softened and the rice is just soft. Add a further 25 g/1 oz butter to the pan and season with salt and pepper to taste. Serve in warm bowls garnished with freshly chopped parsley. Serves 3–4.

TODAY new varieties of 'designer' salad leaves can be found everywhere and we no longer have to have a plain salad of lettuce, tomato and cucumber on our plates. Herbs have always been grown in Britain, but now there is a renewed interest in using them and we are able to buy many more varieties than before, which means we can add interesting twists and flavours to our salads and other dishes. Particularly useful are the herbs sold in pots, which give us a fresh supply for days at a time.

GARDEN SALADS & HERBS

SIMPLE GARDEN SALAD

Take a handful of rocket and trim away any particularly long stems. Pick over a handful of lamb's lettuce and mizuna and tear some leaves of frisée into small pieces. Wash if necessary and make sure they are thoroughly dry. Place the salad leaves in a bowl and add a mixture of herbs, such as parsley, chervil and a few leaves of lemon thyme. Sprinkle over 2–3 tablespoons olive oil and 1 teaspoon freshly squeezed lemon juice and toss to coat the leaves. Add some sea salt crystals and a little pepper, toss again and serve. Serves 4.

TOMATO SALAD

A mixture of tomato varieties in a salad is good as it looks colourful and adds different flavours. Slice 2 beefsteak tomatoes horizontally and cut 4 plum tomatoes into quarters. Cut 12 red cherry tomatoes in half and the same number of gold cherry tomatoes (about 600 g/1 lb 5 oz tomatoes in total). Arrange the tomatoes in a shallow dish, sprinkle with 1/2 teaspoon sea salt and 1/2 teaspoon caster sugar and pour over 5 tablespoons olive oil. Scatter with a good handful of shredded basil and leave to stand for 30 minutes before serving to allow the flavours to mingle. Serves 4.

SPECIAL POTATO SALAD

The first waxy salad potatoes of the season are ideal for making a potato salad. Scrub 800 g/1 lb 12 oz small potatoes (Jersey Royals are my favourite) and cook in boiling salted water for 15–20 minutes until tender. Drain and halve the potatoes while still warm. Place in a serving dish and add 3 tablespoons chopped fresh mixed herbs (parsley, chives, basil and chervil). Pour over 6 tablespoons olive oil and 2 tablespoons white wine, season well with salt and pepper and toss the contents of the dish together. Serve while still warm. If you prefer, you could use a dressing of sour cream or crème fraîche. Serves 4.

GOOD COLESLAW

Shred half a hard white cabbage finely. Grate 2 carrots and core and slice 2 green apples. Chop 2 celery sticks and 3 spring onions finely. Place all the ingredients in a large bowl. In a small bowl, mix together 150 ml/5 fl oz mayonnaise and the same quantity of natural yogurt, add 1 teaspoon French mustard and 1 tablespoon lemon juice and season well with salt and pepper. Pour the dressing over the salad vegetables and mix well. If liked, you could add 40 g/1½ oz raisins and the same amount of chopped walnuts. Serve the coleslaw garnished with a sprinkling of chopped fresh mixed herbs. Serves 4.

7 PERFECT PUDDINGS

There are very few people who claim not to enjoy puddings, but for most of us these recipes are certain to be winners – make sure you make enough for everyone to have seconds! Summer Pudding, with its glorious mix of soft berries, is a real celebration of the season. Its desirability is heightened by the fact that it only appears on menus for a few months a year. Rhubarb Crumble is another seasonal favourite. Try Jam Roly-Poly, Baked Rice Pudding and Bread & Butter Pudding and you'll appreciate why these traditional British puddings remain popular even with changing tastes. And what can be more British than Apple Pie or Sherry Trifle?

JAM ROLY-POLY

A classic British pudding made with suet pastry. This is true rib-sticking stuff – lots of hot gooey pastry and strawberry jam. It needs steaming in a steamer because it is made in the traditional roll shape, not in a basin. A favourite pudding in proper school dinners, a jam roly-poly is always welcome, but particularly on a cold winter's day. A good custard sauce must be served with this pudding. Cream will not do, although a serving of jam sauce goes down well.

SERVES 6

INGREDIENTS
225 g/8 oz self-raising flour
pinch of salt
115 g/4 oz suet
grated rind of 1 lemon
1 tbsp sugar
125 ml/4 fl oz mixed milk and
   water
4–6 tbsp strawberry jam
2 tbsp milk
Custard (see page 172), to serve

1 Sift the flour into a mixing bowl and add the salt and suet. Mix together well. Stir in the lemon rind and the sugar.

2 Make a well in the centre and add the liquid to give a light, elastic dough. Knead lightly until smooth. If you have time, wrap the dough in clingfilm and leave it to rest for 30 minutes.

3 Roll the dough into a 20 x 25-cm/ 8 x 10-inch rectangle.

4 Spread the jam over the dough, leaving a 1-cm/½-inch border. Brush the border with the milk and roll up the dough carefully, like a Swiss roll, from one short end. Seal the ends.

5 Wrap the roly-poly loosely in greaseproof paper and then in foil, sealing the ends well.

6 Prepare a steamer by half filling it with water and putting it on to boil. Place the roly-poly in the steamer and steam over rapidly boiling water for 1½–2 hours, making sure you top up the water from time to time.

7 When cooked, remove from the steamer, unwrap, cut into slices and serve on a warm plate with custard.

VARIATIONS
Use the same amount of mincemeat instead of jam to make a mincemeat roly-poly. Alternatively, use golden syrup instead of the jam and serve with extra hot syrup. Lemon curd or marmalade can also be used.

SPOTTED DICK & CUSTARD

Here's a good old-fashioned pudding, best enjoyed with a proper custard. Suet has been out of favour for a long time, but it's time we started to use it again for good warming dishes when the days are cold and short – there is even a vegetarian version for those who prefer it. The name 'spotted dick' comes from its spotted appearance because the currants or raisins look like spots in the finished pudding. This pudding is traditionally made like a roly-poly, not in the pudding basin shape.

SERVES 6

INGREDIENTS
225 g/8 oz self-raising flour, plus extra for dusting
115 g/4 oz suet
55 g/2 oz caster sugar
140 g/5 oz currants or raisins
grated rind of 1 lemon
150–175 ml/5–6 fl oz milk
2 tsp melted butter, for greasing

CUSTARD
425 ml/15 fl oz single cream
5 egg yolks
3 tbsp caster sugar
½ tsp vanilla extract
1 tsp cornflour (optional)

1 Mix together the flour, suet, sugar, currants and lemon rind in a mixing bowl.

2 Pour in the milk and stir together to give a fairly soft dough.

3 Turn out onto a floured surface and roll into a cylinder. Wrap in greaseproof paper that has been well-buttered and seal the ends, allowing room for the pudding to rise. Overwrap with foil and place in a steamer over a saucepan of boiling water.

4 Steam for about 1–1½ hours, checking the water level in the saucepan from time to time.

5 To make the custard, heat the cream in a small saucepan just to boiling point. Cream the egg yolks, sugar and vanilla extract together in a measuring jug. You can add the cornflour to this cold egg yolk mixture to ensure the sauce does not separate. Pour the hot cream into the jug, stirring all the time. Return the mixture to the saucepan.

6 Heat the custard very gently, stirring constantly, until the sauce has just thickened, then remove from the heat. Alternatively, you can cook the custard in a bowl over a saucepan of simmering water to prevent overcooking.

7 Remove the pudding from the steamer and unwrap. Place on a hot plate and cut into thick slices. Serve with lots of custard.

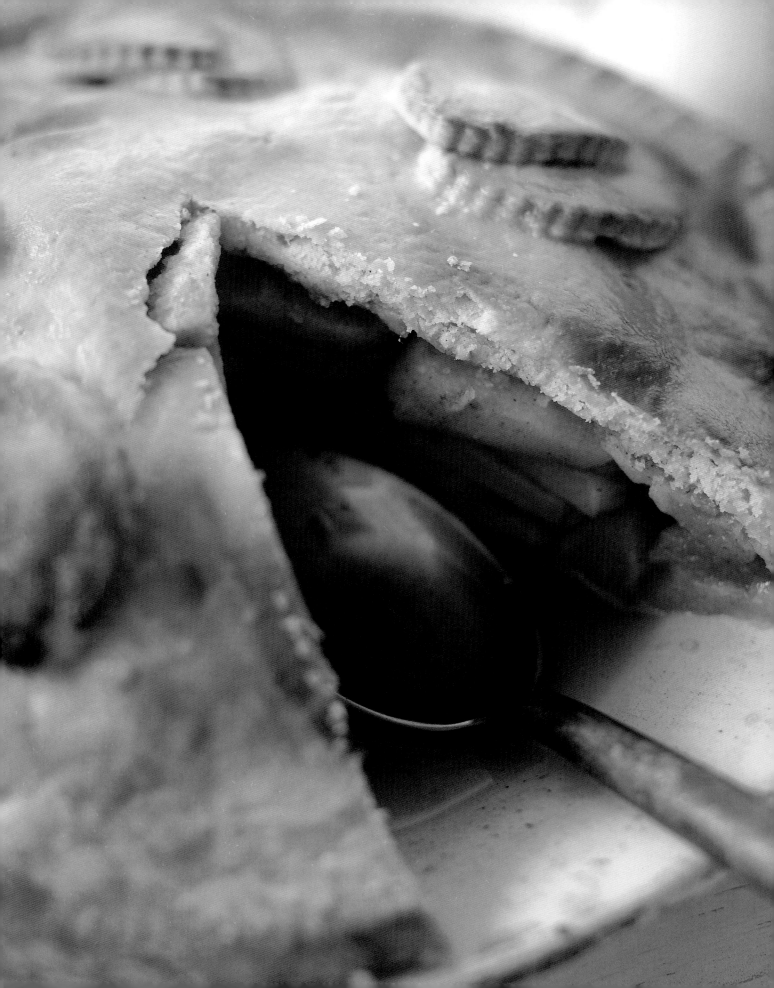

APPLE PIE

Fruit pies are, of course, perennially popular, the most famous of all being our homely apple pie. Many cooks have their own favourite way of preparing apple pie and whether you use a double crust or just a pastry top is purely down to personal choice. You may want to use cooking apples, as here, eating apples or a mixture of both, and the apples can also be flavoured with grated citrus rind. Try adding a handful of blackberries when they appear in the hedgerows in early autumn.

SERVES 6

INGREDIENTS
350 g/12 oz plain flour, plus extra
    for dusting
pinch of salt
85 g/3 oz butter or margarine,
    cut into small pieces
85 g/3 oz lard or white vegetable
    fat, cut into small pieces
about 6 tbsp cold water
1 egg, beaten
Custard (see page 172), to serve

FILLING
750 g–1 kg/1 lb 10 oz–2 lb 4 oz
    cooking apples, peeled, cored
    and sliced
125 g/4½ oz soft light brown or
    caster sugar
½–1 tsp ground cinnamon, mixed
    spice or ground ginger
1–2 tbsp water (optional)

1 To make the pastry, sift the flour and salt into a mixing bowl. Add the butter and fat and rub in with your fingertips until the mixture resembles fine breadcrumbs. Add the water and gather the mixture together into a dough. Wrap the dough in clingfilm and chill in the refrigerator for 30 minutes.

2 Preheat the oven to 220°C/425°F/Gas Mark 7. Roll out almost two thirds of the pastry thinly and use to line a deep 23-cm/9-inch pie plate or pie tin.

3 Mix the apples with the sugar and spice and pack into the pastry case; the filling can come up above the rim. Add the water if needed, particularly if the apples are not very juicy.

4 Roll out the remaining pastry to form a lid. Dampen the edges of the pie rim with water and position the lid, pressing the edges firmly together. Trim and crimp the edges.

5 Use the trimmings to cut out leaves or other shapes to decorate the top of the pie, dampen and attach. Glaze the top of the pie with beaten egg, make 1–2 slits in the top and place the pie on a baking sheet.

6 Bake in the preheated oven for 20 minutes, then reduce the temperature to 180°C/350°F/Gas Mark 4 and bake for a further 30 minutes, or until the pastry is a light golden brown. Serve hot or cold with custard.

STEAMED SYRUP SPONGE

Is this the nation's favourite pudding? A hot pudding steamed to give a light, moist sponge just oozing with syrup. Children and adults alike love it. This recipe can also be followed to make a fruit sponge pudding using a layer of stewed fruit in the basin instead of the syrup. A jam, marmalade or mincemeat pudding can be made in the same way. To make a chocolate pudding, replace 25 g/1 oz flour with cocoa powder and serve with a chocolate sauce – my favourite.

SERVES 6

INGREDIENTS
butter, for greasing
2 tbsp golden syrup, plus extra
  to serve
115 g/4 oz butter
115 g/4 oz caster sugar
2 eggs, lightly beaten
175 g/6 oz self-raising flour
2 tbsp milk
grated rind of 1 lemon

1 Butter a 1.2-litre/2-pint pudding basin and put the syrup into the bottom.

2 Beat together the butter and sugar until soft and creamy, then beat in the eggs, a little at a time.

3 Fold in the flour and stir in the milk to make a soft dropping consistency. Add the lemon rind. Turn the mixture into the pudding basin.

4 Cover the surface with a circle of greaseproof or baking paper and top with a pleated sheet of foil. Secure with some string or crimp the edges of the foil to ensure a tight fit around the basin.

5 Place the pudding in a large saucepan half-filled with boiling water. Cover the saucepan and bring back to the boil over a medium heat. Reduce the heat to a slow simmer and steam for 1½ hours until risen and firm. Keep checking the water level and top up with boiling water as necessary.

6 Remove the pan from the heat and lift out the pudding basin. Remove the cover and loosen the pudding from the sides of the basin using a knife.

7 Turn out into a warmed dish and heat a little more syrup to serve with the pudding.

RHUBARB CRUMBLE

Crumble is one of the simplest puddings, easy to make and delicious to eat. Children enjoy learning how to rub the butter into the flour. Any fruit can be used, but rhubarb is particularly British. The first, forced shoots are the sweetest and the most tender. Ginger is often added to improve the flavour, but I prefer a little orange to add to the taste. The crumble topping can be made with white or wholemeal flour, and some nuts may be added if liked.

SERVES 6

INGREDIENTS
900 g/2 lb rhubarb
115 g/4 oz caster sugar
grated rind and juice of 1 orange
Custard (see page 172), to serve

CRUMBLE TOPPING
225 g/8 oz plain or wholemeal
   flour
115 g/4 oz butter
115 g/4 oz soft brown sugar
1 tsp ground ginger

1 Preheat the oven to 190°C/375°F/ Gas Mark 5.

2 Cut the rhubarb into 2.5-cm/1-inch lengths and place in a 1.7-litre/3-pint ovenproof dish with the sugar and the orange rind and juice.

3 Make the crumble topping by placing the flour in a mixing bowl and rubbing in the butter until the mixture resembles breadcrumbs. Stir in the sugar and the ginger.

4 Spread the crumble topping evenly over the fruit and press down lightly using a fork.

5 Bake in the centre of the oven on a baking tray for 25–30 minutes until the crumble is golden brown.

6 Serve warm with custard.

BAKED RICE PUDDING

Rice pudding is definitely nursery food: some people love it, some loathe it, but it is still a very soothing food. Milk puddings have been popular for centuries and were thought to be good for you. Certainly milk is nourishing, and mixing it with starch and sugar makes a pleasant dish. Other grains like tapioca and semolina can also be used, but are not as popular as rice. The 'skin' is a controversial issue – some discard it, while others fight over it!

SERVES 4–6

INGREDIENTS

1 tbsp melted butter
115 g/4 oz pudding rice
55 g/2 oz caster sugar
850 ml/1½ pints full-cream milk
½ tsp vanilla extract
40 g/1½ oz unsalted butter
whole nutmeg, for grating
jam, to serve

1 Preheat the oven to 150°C/300°F/Gas Mark 2. Grease a 1.2-litre/2-pint baking dish (a gratin dish is good) with the melted butter, place the rice in the dish and sprinkle with the sugar.

2 Heat the milk in a saucepan until almost boiling, then pour over the rice. Add the vanilla extract and stir well to dissolve the sugar.

3 Cut the butter into small pieces and scatter over the surface of the pudding.

4 Grate the whole nutmeg over the top, using as much as you like to give a good covering.

5 Place the dish on a baking tray and bake in the centre of the oven for 1½–2 hours until the pudding is well browned on the top. You can stir it after the first half hour to disperse the rice.

6 Serve hot with jam. It is also good served cold the next day.

VARIATIONS

To make a richer pudding, use half cream and half milk. Other flavours can be used instead of the nutmeg – try grated lemon zest, orange flower water, rosewater, cardamom, cinnamon or mixed spice. Even chocolate can be added, either some chocolate powder added with the milk or roughly chopped pieces sprinkled in towards the end of the cooking time. A tot of rum, brandy or whisky is also good.

BREAD & BUTTER PUDDING

For years bread and butter pudding was poorly regarded because it was often made with dry leftover bread. The resurgence in popularity of the pudding is due to clever cooks using good-quality ingredients and adding fresh eggs and some cream to enrich the pudding, so that it has now become fashionable again in restaurants up and down the country. It can be made with plain bread, malt bread or fruited bread, and the fruit can be varied according to taste.

SERVES 4–6

INGREDIENTS

85 g/3 oz butter, softened
6 slices thick white bread
55 g/2 oz mixed fruit (sultanas, currants and raisins)
25 g/1 oz candied peel
3 large eggs
300 ml/10 fl oz milk
150 ml/5 fl oz double cream
55 g/2 oz caster sugar
whole nutmeg, for grating
1 tbsp demerara sugar
cream, to serve

1 Preheat the oven to 180°C/350°F/Gas Mark 4.

2 Use a little of the butter to grease a 20 x 25-cm/8 x 10-inch baking dish and the remainder to butter the slices of bread. Cut the bread into quarters and arrange half overlapping in the dish.

3 Scatter half the fruit and peel over the bread, cover with the remaining bread slices and add the remaining fruit and peel.

4 In a mixing jug, whisk the eggs well and mix in the milk, cream and sugar. Pour this over the pudding and leave to stand for 15 minutes to allow the bread to soak up some of the egg mixture. Tuck in most of the fruit as you don't want it to burn in the oven. Grate the nutmeg over the top of the pudding, according to taste, and sprinkle over the demerara sugar.

5 Place the pudding on a baking tray and bake at the top of the oven for 30–40 minutes until just set and golden brown.

6 Remove from the oven and serve warm with a little pouring cream.

VARIATIONS
You can use dried apricots instead of the mixed fruit and spread a little apricot jam on the buttered bread. Alternatively, add a sliced banana to the pudding and sprinkle with a little cinnamon or add sliced pears and use slices of panettone, adding some vanilla extract to the egg mixture. For a grown-up pudding, pour a small glass of rum or whisky into the egg mixture.

QUEEN OF PUDDINGS

This was a very popular pudding on feast days and holidays. It looks very exotic, yet is simply made from breadcrumbs, eggs and milk, then topped with jam and meringue, which make it delicious and indulgent! You can make it using fruit instead of jam – a layer of apple purée or fresh raspberries is good – and a few flaked almonds scattered over the meringue before cooking make a lovely crunchy addition. I like to serve these puddings in individual dishes for dinner parties.

SERVES 4–6

INGREDIENTS
2 tbsp butter
600 ml/1 pint milk
115 g/4 oz fresh white
  breadcrumbs
115 g/4 oz caster sugar
grated rind of 1 lemon
3 eggs, separated
3 tbsp raspberry jam, warmed
1 tsp golden granulated sugar

1 Preheat the oven to 180°C/350°F/ Gas Mark 4.

2 Using a little of the butter, grease a 1-litre/1¾-pint baking dish.

3 Heat the remaining butter in the saucepan with the milk and gently bring to the boil over a medium heat.

4 Remove from the heat and stir in the breadcrumbs, 1 tablespoon of the caster sugar and the lemon rind.

5 Allow to stand and cool for 15 minutes, then beat in the egg yolks.

6 Pour the mixture into the baking dish, smooth the surface and bake in the centre of the oven for about 30 minutes until it is set. Spread over the jam.

7 Whisk the egg whites in the mixing bowl until very thick, then gradually add the remaining caster sugar. Continue until all the sugar has been added.

8 Spoon the meringue over the pudding and make sure the meringue covers it completely. Swirl the meringue into attractive peaks and sprinkle with the granulated sugar.

9 Bake again in the centre of the oven for 10–15 minutes until the meringue is golden brown but still soft. Serve warm.

BAKEWELL TART

Originally called Bakewell pie or Bakewell pudding, this Derbyshire tart is one of the stars of the British pudding repertoire. A rich almond-cream mixture baked over a thin layer of strawberry jam in a crisp, buttery crust makes this tart quite irresistible. The pastry is very rich and can be difficult to roll out. Rather than adding extra flour, gently roll it out between two sheets of clingfilm. Peel off the top sheet of clingfilm, then invert the pastry into the flan tin and peel off the other sheet.

SERVES 4

INGREDIENTS

PASTRY
155 g/5½ oz plain flour, plus extra for dusting
85 g/3 oz butter, cut into small pieces, plus extra for greasing
35 g/1¼ oz icing sugar, sifted
finely grated rind of ½ lemon
½ egg yolk, beaten
1½ tbsp milk
4 tbsp strawberry jam

FILLING
100 g/3½ oz butter
100 g/3½ oz soft light brown sugar
2 eggs, beaten
1 tsp almond essence
75 g/2¾ oz ground rice
3 tbsp ground almonds
3 tbsp flaked almonds, toasted
icing sugar, to decorate

1 To make the pastry, sift the flour into a bowl. Rub in the butter with your fingertips until the mixture resembles fine breadcrumbs. Mix in the icing sugar, lemon rind, egg yolk and milk.

2 Knead briefly on a lightly floured work surface. Wrap the dough in clingfilm and chill in the refrigerator for 30 minutes.

3 Preheat the oven to 190°C/375°F/ Gas Mark 5. Grease a 20-cm/8-inch ovenproof flan tin. Roll out the pastry to a thickness of 5 mm/¼ inch and use it to line the base and side of the tin. Prick all over the base with a fork, then spread with the jam.

4 To make the filling, cream the butter and sugar together until fluffy. Gradually beat in the eggs, followed by the almond essence, ground rice and almonds. Spread the mixture evenly over the jam-covered pastry, then sprinkle over the flaked almonds. Bake in the oven for 40 minutes, until golden. Remove from the oven, dust with icing sugar and serve warm.

SHERRY TRIFLE

Trifle always includes cake soaked in sherry, some fruit, custard and cream. A proper custard is called for, but if time is short, you can cheat by using one of the freshly prepared chilled custards available now, which are really good. Any fruit can be used, fresh or canned, and the topping should be whipped cream. The traditional decoration is hundreds and thousands but if you have used really good ingredients I would suggest some whole toasted almonds or silver dragées.

SERVES 6–8

INGREDIENTS

8 trifle sponges or 1 layer of Victoria Sandwich Cake (see page 204)
115 g/4 oz raspberry jam
150 ml/5 fl oz sherry
55 g/2 oz small macaroons or ratafia biscuits
2 tbsp brandy
350 g/12 oz raspberries, fresh or frozen
600 ml/1 pint custard, cooled
300 ml/10 fl oz double cream
2 tbsp milk
40 g/1½ oz toasted flaked almonds or silver dragées, to decorate

1 Break the sponges or cake into pieces and spread with the jam.

2 Place in a large glass serving bowl and pour over the sherry.

3 Add the macaroons to the bowl and sprinkle over the brandy.

4 Spoon the raspberries on top.

5 Pour over the custard, cover the bowl with clingfilm and leave to settle for 2–3 hours or overnight.

6 Just before serving, whip the cream with the milk until it is thick but still soft. Spoon over the custard and swirl around using a knife to give an attractive appearance. Decorate as desired with almonds or dragées and serve.

VARIATIONS
You can use Syllabub (see page 193) as a topping and omit the custard and cream. Alternatively, a 'Black Forest' trifle can be made using Morello cherry jam and chocolate cake. Black cherries (fresh or canned) may be used in place of the raspberries and the top of the trifle decorated with 2 tablespoons grated chocolate.

SUMMER PUDDING

This is one of the few uncooked puddings. It is made in the traditional pudding shape with bread and a variety of summer fruits – hence the name. This pudding was devised in the nineteenth century as an invalid food when pastry was considered too rich for convalescents. You can vary the fruits according to what is available, but it is not a good idea to use strawberries because they are too soft. In the autumn, a similar pudding can be made using stewed apples and blackberries.

SERVES 6

INGREDIENTS
675 g/1 lb 8 oz mixed soft
  fruits, such as redcurrants,
  blackcurrants, raspberries and
  blackberries
140 g/5 oz caster sugar
2 tbsp crème de framboise
  liqueur (optional)
6–8 slices good day-old white
  bread, crusts removed
icing sugar, for dusting (optional)
double cream, to serve

1 You will need an 850-ml/1½-pint pudding basin.

2 Place the fruits in a large saucepan with the sugar.

3 Over a low heat, very slowly bring to the boil, stirring carefully to ensure that the sugar has dissolved. Cook over a low heat for only 2–3 minutes until the juices run but the fruit still holds its shape. Add the liqueur, if using.

4 Line the pudding basin with some of the slices of bread (cut them to shape so that the bread fits well). Spoon in the cooked fruit and juices, reserving a little of the juice for later.

5 Cover the surface of the fruit with the remaining bread. Place a saucer on top of the pudding and weight it down for at least 8 hours or overnight in the refrigerator.

6 Turn out the pudding and pour over the reserved juices to colour any white bits of bread that may be showing. Sprinkle with the icing sugar, if using, and serve with cream.

SYLLABUB

In the Middle Ages, the cream and wine confection now called a syllabub was sometimes called a 'flummery' or 'posset'. It is alleged that originally the cow was milked directly into a jug of wine to make a froth or foam. Through time, the foam has become more important than the drink and a thicker dessert has evolved. Wine or sherry can be used depending on the sweetness required. Some syllabubs separate after several hours; this one keeps its solid state for a day.

SERVES 4–6

INGREDIENTS
grated rind and juice of 1 lemon
125 ml/4 fl oz sweet white wine
2 tbsp brandy
55 g/2 oz caster sugar
300 ml/10 fl oz double cream
zest of 1 lemon, to decorate
sponge fingers or ratafia biscuits,
  to serve

1 Place the rind and the juice of the lemon in a bowl together with the wine and brandy. Cover and leave to infuse for a few hours or overnight.

2 Stir in the sugar until it has dissolved.

3 Whip the cream in a large bowl using an electric mixer. When it starts to thicken, carefully pour in the liquid, a little at a time, until it is all mixed in. The mixture should be very thick and soft, do not overwhip it.

4 Spoon into small glasses and chill for a few hours. This can be made a day ahead.

5 Decorate with the lemon zest sprinkled on top. Sponge fingers or ratafia biscuits can be served with the dessert.

VARIATIONS
Syllabub can be made with cassis or crème de framboise to give a pretty pink colour. It can also be layered with fruit such as raspberries.

ETON MESS

This delectable dessert is from a very traditional British background: Eton College. On the fourth of June every year there is a celebration at the school and this dessert is always served. It is a sort of strawberry fool, which started out as a simple concoction of strawberries and cream flavoured with sugar and vanilla, mixed together to give a 'mess'. Today the recipe has developed into a richer, truly wonderful 'mess' of strawberries, cream and crushed meringue.

SERVES 4–6

INGREDIENTS
3 egg whites
175 g/6 oz caster sugar
700 g/1 lb 9 oz strawberries
2 tbsp icing sugar
2 tbsp crème de fraise
   (strawberry) liqueur (optional)
300 ml/10 fl oz double cream
150 ml/5 fl oz single cream

1 Preheat the oven to 150°C/300°F/ Gas Mark 2.

2 Whisk the egg whites in a mixing bowl using an electric mixer until thick and in soft peaks. Add the sugar gradually, whisking well with each addition. The meringue mixture should be glossy and firm.

3 Spoon the meringue onto a baking tray lined with baking paper and spread into a rough 30-cm/12-inch round. Cook for 45–50 minutes until the meringue is firm on the outside but still soft in the centre. Remove from the oven and allow to cool.

4 Check over the strawberries and hull them.

5 Place a third of the berries (choose the larger ones) in a liquidizer and purée with the icing sugar. Pour the purée into a bowl, add the liqueur, if using, and the remaining strawberries and turn them in the sauce until well mixed.

6 Whip together the double and single cream until thick but still light and floppy.

7 Break the meringue into large pieces and place half in a large glass serving bowl. Spoon over half the fruit mixture and half the cream. Layer up the remaining ingredients and lightly fold the mixtures together so you have a streaky appearance.

8 Serve soon after mixing or the meringues will soften.

8 AFTERNOON TEA

Nothing can be more British than an afternoon cuppa with a sweet or savoury bite to take the edge off your appetite until it's time for the evening meal. It's easy to just buy Tea Cakes, Crumpets, English Muffins and Eccles Cakes, but there's no reason not to make your own. Scones, warm from the oven, and Victoria Sandwich Cake are easy-to-make teatime treats, but you can add variety to your tea table with Shortbread, Gingerbread, Irish Soda Bread and Welsh Bara Brith. Finally, few touches are more appreciated at teatime than home-made preserves – pots of your own Raspberry Jam and Lemon Curd will bring praise all round.

SCONES

Scones are quick to make and are delicious served freshly baked. Originally from Scotland, scones are now associated with afternoon tea all over Britain, particularly in Devon where the 'cream tea' (scones, jam and clotted cream) is served in all the tea shops. Scones can be made with or without fruit and savoury scones, made with a little grated cheese, are also popular and can be served with various fillings as a good alternative to sandwiches.

MAKES 10–12

INGREDIENTS
450 g/1 lb plain flour, plus extra
   for dusting
½ tsp salt
2 tsp baking powder
55 g/2 oz butter
2 tbsp caster sugar
250 ml/9 fl oz milk
3 tbsp milk, for glazing
strawberry jam and clotted
   cream, to serve

1 Preheat the oven to 220°C/425°F/Gas Mark 7.

2 Sift the flour, salt and baking powder into a bowl. Rub in the butter until the mixture resembles breadcrumbs. Stir in the sugar.

3 Make a well in the centre and pour in the milk. Stir in using a round-bladed knife and make a soft dough.

4 Turn the mixture onto a floured surface and lightly flatten the dough until it is of an even thickness, about 1 cm/½ inch. Don't be heavy-handed – scones need a light touch.

5 Use a 6-cm/2½-inch pastry cutter to cut out the scones and place on the baking tray.

6 Glaze with a little milk and bake for 10–12 minutes, until golden and well risen.

7 Cool on a wire rack and serve freshly baked with strawberry jam and clotted cream.

VARIATIONS
To make fruit scones, add 55 g/2 oz mixed fruit with the sugar. To make wholemeal scones, use wholemeal flour and omit the sugar. These are delicious to serve with soup or as an accompaniment to cheese. To make cheese scones, omit the sugar and add 55 g/2 oz finely grated Cheddar or Double Gloucester cheese to the mixture with 1 teaspoon mustard.

TEA CAKES

Tea cakes are the basis of a proper English tea. Afternoon tea was reputed to have been started by the Duchess of Bedford. In the nineteenth century dinner was eaten later in the evening, so she began to order sweetmeats and slices of bread and butter in the afternoon. In our own times, tea in a department store café, gallery, museum or hotel often includes tea cakes. They are made from bread dough enriched with sugar, butter and dried fruit and are usually toasted.

MAKES 10–12

INGREDIENTS
300 ml/10 fl oz milk
4 tsp dried yeast
55 g/2 oz caster sugar
450 g/1 lb strong plain flour, plus
   extra for dusting
1 tsp salt
1 tsp ground mixed spice
115 g/4 oz currants
25 g/1 oz mixed peel, chopped
55 g/2 oz butter, melted
1 egg, beaten
sugar glaze made from 2 tbsp
   sugar and 2 tbsp warm milk

1 Warm the milk in a saucepan until just tepid and add the yeast with 1 teaspoon of the sugar. Mix well and allow to froth in a warm place for 15 minutes.

2 Sift the flour, salt and spice into a large mixing bowl and add the currants, peel and the remaining sugar.

3 Make a well in the centre of the dry ingredients and pour in the milk mixture, the melted butter and egg.

4 Mix well using a wooden spoon at first and then by hand.

5 Turn out onto a lightly floured surface and knead lightly until the dough is smooth and elastic.

6 Put the dough back into the bowl, cover with clingfilm and leave to rise in a warm place for 40–45 minutes until it has doubled in size.

7 Knead the dough again lightly and divide into 10–12 even-sized buns, shaping well.

8 Preheat the oven to 220°C/425°F/Gas Mark 7.

9 Place the buns on two greased baking trays, cover with a damp tea towel or large plastic bags and allow to rise again for 30–40 minutes.

10 Bake the tea cakes in the oven for 18–20 minutes until they are golden brown. Remove from the oven, place on a wire rack and glaze with the sugar glaze while still hot. Serve lightly toasted.

CRUMPETS

Crumpets have always been associated with winter firesides and tea time and there is nothing nicer than to sit by a roaring fire with a toasting fork in your hand toasting crumpets. Spreading them with lots of butter until it drips through to your fingers is also part of enjoying crumpets. In some parts of England and in Wales they are better known as pikelets. Crumpets are now readily available, but to make them at home is a magical experience as the traditional 'bubble' appearance develops.

MAKES 10–12

INGREDIENTS
350 g/12 oz plain flour
pinch of salt
15 g/½ oz fresh yeast
1 tsp caster sugar
400 ml/14 fl oz tepid milk
2 tbsp butter, plus extra to serve

1 Place the flour and salt in a mixing bowl and mix together. Blend the fresh yeast with the sugar in a basin and add the milk.

2 Pour the liquid onto the flour and mix everything together until the batter is smooth, beating the batter thoroughly so that it is light and airy. Cover and leave to rise in a warm place for 1 hour until well risen.

3 Stir the batter to knock out any air and check the consistency. If it is too thick, add 1 tablespoon of water (it should look rather gloopy). Leave aside for 10 minutes.

4 Grease a frying pan and 4 crumpet rings or 7.5-cm/3-inch plain cutters with the butter. Place the frying pan over a medium heat and leave to heat up for 2 minutes. Arrange the rings in the pan and spoon in enough batter to come halfway up each ring. Cook over a low heat for 5–6 minutes until small holes begin to appear and the top is starting to dry.

5 Remove the crumpet rings with a palette knife or an oven glove. Turn the crumpets over (the base should be golden brown) and cook the top for just 1–2 minutes to cook through.

6 Keep the first batch of crumpets warm while you cook the rest of the batter.

7 Serve freshly cooked with butter or, if you want to serve them later, allow them to cool and reheat in a toaster or by the fire.

VICTORIA SANDWICH CAKE

It is said that this was the favourite cake of Queen Victoria. It is sometimes called a sponge cake, but a sponge contains no fat and one of the most important ingredients of this cake is good butter. The cake is traditionally made by the creaming method, although today you can easily make it by the all-in-one method – just make sure the butter is softened, add 1 teaspoon of baking powder to the flour and then beat all the ingredients together with an electric mixer.

SERVESS 8–10

INGREDIENTS
175 g/6 oz butter, at room temperature, plus extra for greasing
175 g/6 oz caster sugar
3 eggs, beaten
175 g/6 oz self-raising flour
pinch of salt

TO SERVE
3 tbsp raspberry jam
1 tbsp caster or icing sugar

1 Preheat the oven to 180°C/350°F/ Gas Mark 4.

2 Grease two 20-cm/8-inch sponge tins and base-line with greaseproof paper or baking paper.

3 Cream the butter and sugar together in a mixing bowl using a wooden spoon or a hand-held mixer until the mixture is pale in colour and light and fluffy.

4 Add the egg a little at a time, beating well after each addition.

5 Sift the flour and salt and carefully add to the mixture, folding it in with a metal spoon or a spatula.

6 Divide the mixture between the tins and smooth over with the spatula.

7 Place them on the same shelf in the centre of the oven and bake for 25–30 minutes until well risen, golden brown and beginning to shrink from the sides of the tin.

8 Remove from the oven and allow to stand for 1 minute.

9 Loosen the cakes from around the edge of the tins using a palette knife. Turn the cakes out onto a clean tea towel, remove the paper and invert them onto a wire rack (this prevents the wire rack from marking the top of the cakes). When completely cool, sandwich together with the jam and sprinkle with the sugar. The cake is delicious when freshly baked, but any remaining cake can be stored in an airtight tin for up to 1 week.

ECCLES CAKES

Eccles cakes come from the small town of Eccles near Manchester. They were devised by the niece of Elizabeth Raffald, who was a well-known cook in the area. Being a Lancastrian, these are the first sort of cakes I was allowed to make. My aunt would do all her baking on a certain day and at the end of the session, I would be able to make Eccles cakes with her leftover flaky or puff pastry. The filling would be any leftover fruit mixed with butter and brown sugar and sometimes some spices.

MAKES 10–12

INGREDIENTS

400 g/14 oz ready-made puff pastry
2 tbsp plain flour, for dusting
55 g/2 oz butter, softened, plus extra for greasing
55 g/2 oz soft brown sugar
85 g/3 oz currants
25 g/1 oz mixed peel, chopped
½ tsp ground mixed spice (optional)
1 egg white, lightly beaten
1–2 tsp caster sugar

1 Preheat the oven to 220°C/425°F/Gas Mark 7.

2 Roll out the pastry thinly, using the flour to dust the work surface and the rolling pin.

3 Cut into rounds using a 9-cm/3½-inch cutter. Fold the trimmings carefully, re-roll and repeat the cuttings to give a total of 10–12 rounds.

4 In a basin, mix together the butter and soft brown sugar until creamy, then add the dried fruit and mixed spice, if using.

5 Put a teaspoon of the filling in the centre of each pastry round. Draw the edges of the circles together and pinch the edges over the filling. Reshape each cake into a round.

6 Turn the cakes over and lightly roll them with the rolling pin until the currants just show through. Score several slits into each cake with a knife.

7 Place the cakes on a greased baking tray and allow to rest for 10–15 minutes.

8 Brush the cakes with the egg white, sprinkle with 1 teaspoon of the caster sugar and bake at the top of the oven for about 15 minutes until golden brown and crisp.

9 Transfer to a wire rack and sprinkle with a little more sugar, if desired. Delicious straight from the oven, they also keep well in an airtight tin for a week and can be reheated before serving.

SHORTBREAD

Shortbread dates back at least to the sixteenth century, when it was known to be a favourite of Mary Queen of Scots. It is ideal for teatime, morning coffee, or as an accompaniment to desserts. The formula for shortbread is one part sugar and two parts butter to three parts flour. The sugar used is usually caster, the butter slightly salted, and the flour plain white, though a tablespoon of semolina, rice flour or cornflour may replace some of the flour to give a different texture.

MAKES 8 PIECES

INGREDIENTS

Butter, for greasing
175 g/6 oz plain flour, plus 1 tbsp for dusting
Pinch of salt
55 g/2 oz caster sugar
115 g/4 oz butter, cut into small pieces
1 tsp golden caster sugar

1 Grease a 20-cm/8-inch fluted cake tin or flan tin.

2 Preheat the oven to 150°C/300°F/Gas Mark 2.

3 Mix together the flour, salt and sugar. Rub the butter into the dry ingredients. Continue to work the mixture until it forms a soft dough. Make sure you do not overwork the shortbread or it will be tough, not crumbly as it should be.

4 Lightly press the dough into the cake tin. If you don't have a fluted tin, roll out the dough on a lightly floured board, place on a baking tray and pinch the edges to form a scalloped pattern.

5 Mark into 8 pieces with a knife. Prick all over with a fork and bake in the centre of the oven for 45–50 minutes until the shortbread is firm and just coloured.

6 Allow to cool in the tin and dredge with the sugar. Cut into portions and remove to a wire rack. Store in an airtight container in a cool place until needed.

GINGERBREAD

Spices have been used in sweet recipes throughout history and ginger is one of the favourites. A sticky gingerbread is a wonderful cake to serve at teatime, but is also useful for packed lunches and picnics and, like its oatmeal cousin parkin, is traditionally served on Guy Fawkes Night around the bonfire. Gingerbread includes a lot of sugar, syrup and treacle, which makes it a good keeping cake, and it is worthwhile making a large quantity because it will keep for 2–3 weeks in an airtight tin.

MAKES 12–16 PIECES

INGREDIENTS
450 g/1 lb plain flour
3 tsp baking powder
1 tsp bicarbonate of soda
3 tsp ground ginger
175 g/6 oz butter
175 g/6 oz soft brown sugar
175 g/6 oz black treacle
175 g/6 oz golden syrup
1 egg, beaten
300 ml/10 fl oz milk
cream or warmed golden syrup,
   to serve

1 Line a 23-cm/9-inch square cake tin, 5 cm/2 inches deep, with greaseproof or baking paper.

2 Preheat the oven to 160°C/325°F/Gas Mark 3.

3 Sift the dry ingredients into a large mixing bowl.

4 Place the butter, sugar, treacle and syrup in a medium saucepan and heat over a low heat until the butter has melted and the sugar dissolved. Allow to cool a little.

5 Mix the beaten egg with the milk and add to the cooled syrup mixture.

6 Add all the liquid ingredients to the flour mixture and beat well using a wooden spoon until the mixture is smooth and glossy.

7 Pour the mixture into the prepared tin and bake in the centre of the oven for 1½ hours until well risen and just firm to the touch. A skewer inserted into the cake should come out cleanly if it is cooked. This gives a lovely sticky gingerbread, but if you like a firmer cake cook for a further 15 minutes.

8 Remove from the oven and allow the cake to cool in the tin. When cool, remove the cake from the tin with the lining paper. Overwrap with foil and place in an airtight tin for up to 1 week to allow the flavours to mature.

9 Cut into wedges and serve for tea or serve with cream as a pudding. Extra warmed syrup is an added extravagance.

BARA BRITH

Tea breads are popular all over the British Isles and there are many of them. They are traditionally made using yeast and are flavoured with fruits and spices. Today, some tea breads are made not with yeast but using bicarbonate of soda or baking powder as a raising agent, but the original recipe using yeast is the best. The Welsh name 'bara brith' means 'speckled bread' and is similar to the Irish barm brack. Serve this in thin slices spread with butter.

MAKES 1 LOAF

INGREDIENTS
butter, for greasing
175 ml/6 fl oz milk
4 tsp dried yeast
115 g/4 oz brown sugar
450 g/1 lb strong plain flour,
  plus extra for dusting
½ tsp salt
115 g/4 oz butter, plus extra
  to serve
280 g/10 oz mixed dried fruit
  (sultanas, currants and raisins)
55 g/2 oz mixed peel
1 tsp ground mixed spice
1 egg, beaten

1 Grease a 900-g/2-lb loaf tin.

2 Warm the milk in a saucepan until tepid and add the yeast with 1 teaspoon of the sugar. Mix well and allow to froth in a warm place for 15 minutes.

3 Sift the flour and salt into a mixing bowl. Rub the butter into the flour mixture until it resembles breadcrumbs then add the remaining sugar, dried fruit, peel and mixed spice and stir well. Add the beaten egg and the frothy yeast mixture and mix to form a soft dough.

4 Turn the mixture out onto a floured surface and knead until smooth. Replace the dough in the bowl, cover with clingfilm and leave in a warm place to rise for 1–1½ hours until it has doubled in bulk.

5 Preheat the oven to 190°C/375°F/Gas Mark 5.

6 Turn the dough out again and knead lightly. Shape the dough into a rectangle the length of the tin and 3 times the width. Fold the dough into 3 lengthwise and put it in the tin with the join underneath. Cover and leave to rise in a warm place for 30–40 minutes, until it has risen above the tin.

7 Bake towards the bottom of the oven for 30 minutes. Turn the loaf around and cover the top with foil if it is getting too brown. Continue to cook for a further 30 minutes.

8 Turn the loaf out of the tin and tap it on the bottom. If cooked it will sound hollow. If not fully cooked, return it to the oven for a further 10 minutes (without the tin). Leave to cool on a wire rack. Serve cut into slices and spread with butter.

SODA BREAD

Soda bread has been a staple in Ireland for many centuries. It is a bread made without yeast, the raising agent being bicarbonate of soda mixed with buttermilk. It is simple to make, needs very little kneading and no time at all rising. The loaves are cut on the top into a cross shape to help the bread rise and, according to Irish folklore, to let the devils (or the fairies) out. Soda bread can be made with brown or white flour or a mixture of the two and is a wonderful partner for cheese.

ERVES 4–6

INGREDIENTS
50 g/1 lb plain flour, plus extra
for dusting
tsp salt
tsp bicarbonate of soda
00 ml/14 fl oz buttermilk

1 Preheat the oven to 220°C/425°F/Gas Mark 7.

2 Sift the flour, salt and bicarbonate of soda into a mixing bowl.

3 Make a well in the centre of the dry ingredients and pour in most of the buttermilk.

4 Mix well together using your hands. The dough should be very soft but not too wet. If necessary, add the remaining buttermilk.

5 Turn the dough out onto a floured surface and knead it lightly. Shape into a 20-cm/8-inch round.

6 Place the bread on a greased baking tray, cut a cross in the top and bake in the oven for 25–30 minutes. When done it should sound hollow if tapped on the bottom. Eat while still warm. Soda bread is always best eaten the same day as it is made.

ENGLISH MUFFINS

English muffins are somewhat reminiscent of Dickens novels: cold winter snow scenes and roaring log fires spied through a frosty window. Muffins were sold hot on the streets of London in the nineteenth century. The English muffin is a light, yeast-based, enriched bread, which is cooked on a griddle to give a crunchy top and bottom with a soft inside. They should be split while hot, a piece of butter placed in the centre and pressed back together again before eating immediately.

MAKES 10–12

INGREDIENTS

2 x 7 g/¼ oz sachets easy-blend dried yeast
250 ml/9 fl oz tepid water
125 ml/4 fl oz natural yogurt
450 g/1 lb strong plain flour, plus extra for dusting
½ tsp salt
50 g/1¾ oz fine semolina
oil, for greasing
butter and/or jam, to serve

1 Mix the yeast with half the tepid water in a bowl until it has dissolved.

2 Add the remaining water and the yogurt and mix well.

3 Sieve the flour into a large bowl and add the salt. Pour in the yeast liquid and mix well to a soft dough.

4 Turn out onto a floured surface and knead well until very smooth. Put the dough back into the bowl, cover with clingfilm and leave to rise for 30–40 minutes in a warm place until it has doubled in size.

5 Turn out again onto the surface and knead lightly. Roll out the dough to a thickness of 2 cm/¾ inch.

6 Using a 7.5-cm/3-inch cutter, cut into rounds and scatter the semolina over each muffin. Re-roll the trimmings of the dough and make further muffins until it is all used up. Place them on a lightly floured baking tray, cover and allow to rise again for 30–40 minutes.

7 Heat a griddle or a large frying pan and lightly grease with a little oil. Cook half the muffins for 7–8 minutes on each side, taking care not to burn them. Repeat with the rest of the muffins.

8 Serve freshly cooked with lots of butter. Muffins can be kept for 2 days in an airtight tin. To reheat, split them across the centre and quickly toast them before serving with butter and jam.

RASPBERRY JAM

Jam-making at home is sadly a dying art. Just try making a small quantity and you will be surprised how easy it is and what a superior product you can achieve. Strawberry jam is probably Britain's favourite, but it is a little difficult to make satisfactorily because strawberries don't contain enough pectin to make a firm set. A simpler one to make is raspberry because it sets easily. Use it on scones or hot buttered toast, but also to fill a Victoria sandwich cake, in a trifle and as a sauce over ice cream.

MAKES 5 X 450-G/1-LB JARS

INGREDIENTS
1.3 kg/3 lb raspberries
1.3 kg/3 lb granulated or
  preserving sugar

1 You will need 5 x 450 g/1 lb jam jars with lids and waxed discs. To sterilize the jars, make sure they are washed in soapy water and rinsed well and then heat in a moderate oven for 5 minutes.

2 Put the fruit into a large saucepan and slowly cook until some of the juices begin to run. Simmer gently for 15–20 minutes until tender. Add the sugar and stir until dissolved.

3 Raise the heat and boil hard for 2–3 minutes until setting point is reached. Test by using a sugar thermometer: when it reads 105°C/221°F it is at a good setting point. Alternatively, test by dropping a small spoonful of jam onto a cold saucer, refrigerate to cool, then push it with a clean finger. If it forms a wrinkled skin it is ready. If not, boil the jam for 1 further minute and repeat.

4 Remove the pan from the heat and allow to cool for 2 minutes, skimming if necessary.

5 Have the jars warmed in a moderate oven and fill carefully using a ladle and a jam funnel. Top with the waxed discs and screw on the lids. Wipe the jars clean and leave to cool. Label and date to avoid confusion later.

6 Store in a cool, dry place. Once opened the jam will keep for up to 2 months in the refrigerator.

LEMON CURD

Lemon curd is a delicious preserve that is useful to make during the spring months when there is no particular fruit in season. It is easy to make and best eaten fresh, but it can be stored for up to 2 months in the refrigerator. Orange curd can also be made using Seville oranges when in season (January and February) and a lime curd can be made for those who prefer a slightly sharper spread. Use on buttered scones, to fill a Victoria sandwich cake or to make luscious lemon tarts.

MAKES 700 G/1 LB 9 OZ

INGREDIENTS
unwaxed lemons
50 g/12 oz caster sugar
eggs, beaten
75 g/6 oz butter

1 You will need 2 jam jars or 3–4 small jars with lids and waxed discs. To sterilize the jars, make sure they are washed in soapy water and rinsed well and then heat in a moderate oven for 5 minutes.

2 Carefully grate the rind from each of the lemons using a fine grater. Make sure you only take the yellow rind and not the bitter white pith.

3 Cut the lemons in half and squeeze out all the juice, then sieve to remove the pips.

4 Place a medium heatproof bowl over a saucepan of simmering water and add the lemon rind, juice and sugar. Mix together well until the sugar has dissolved.

5 Add the eggs and the butter cut into small pieces and continue to stir for 25–30 minutes until the butter has melted and the mixture begins to thicken. Beat well and turn into the jars. Cover and label before storing. Once opened the lemon curd will keep for up to 2 months in the refrigerator.

VARIATIONS
make orange curd, use
Seville oranges instead of the
lemons, and for lime prepare
limes for the same amount
the other ingredients.
Blackberries and blackcurrants
can also be made into curd by
stewing the fruit first and sieving
make a purée.